Strategic Reward and Recognition

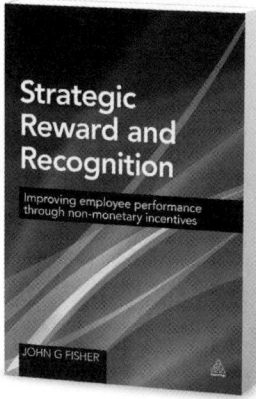

Strategic Reward and Recognition

Improving employee performance through non-monetary incentives

John G Fisher

KoganPage

LONDON PHILADELPHIA NEW DELHI

First published in Great Britain and the United States in 2015 by Kogan Page Limited

2nd Floor, 45 Gee Street
London
EC1V 3RS
United Kingdom

1518 Walnut Street, Suite 1100
Philadelphia PA 19102
USA

4737/23 Ansari Road
Daryaganj
New Delhi 110002
India

© John G Fisher, 2015

The right of John G Fisher to be identified as the author of this work has been asserted by him in accordance with the Copyright, Designs and Patents Act 1988.

ISBN   978 0 7494 7252 8
E-ISBN 978 0 7494 7253 5

British Library Cataloguing-in-Publication Data

A CIP record for this book is available from the British Library.

Library of Congress Control Number
2015015460

Typeset by Amnet
Print production managed by Jellyfish
Printed and bound in Great Britain by CPI Group (UK) Ltd, Croydon CR0 4YY

CONTENTS

ACKNOWLEDGEMENTS

I would like to thank the following organizations for their specific help, input and contributions of all kinds for this book about reward and recognition: BI Inc, Fast Future, Fiat, FMI Group, HR Magazine, Human Capital Institute, Incentive Federation, Incentive Performance Center, Indesit, Institute of Promotional Marketing, P&MM and Pinsent Masons. There are many individuals who also contributed to this book through discussion, experience and know-how to help me make sense of what reward and recognition are. But there are too many individuals who were extraordinarily generous with their time for me to acknowledge by name. They know who they are and I am very grateful.

Any misunderstandings, errors and misinterpretations, however, are entirely my own.

Introduction
Dealing with human beings

For too long now organizations have seen the 'problem' of employee or business partner motivation being solved by mechanical means. It would appear that by introducing some kind of non-monetary reward or recognition scheme the sponsor can change human behaviour at work in a quick, predictable way. But no sooner are such programmes introduced than unexpected results happen. They stop working.

So another programme is needed to patch up the initial plan. And then another. And then another. What starts out as an ambition to achieve a fully integrated people motivation programme often results in conflicting activities that cancel each other out. Confusion abounds. Participants ignore the numerous, stop–start messages and carry on with their day-to-day business, as usual. No one wants to appear ungrateful, but why can't they just leave us alone to get on with our jobs?, they cry.

In this book I will review what produces an effective and sustainable reward and recognition programme, whether your organization is a multinational conglomerate or a local engineering supplier. We start with what human motivation within a corporate or non-profit organization context looks like and what the theories tell us about applying the principles to modern organizations.

We will then explore the four key elements of a performance improvement programme (PIP): research, skills development, communication and rewards/incentives. In particular you need to know about the different types of recognition programmes and reward options so that you can make the right choices for your specific employee or distributor participant profile. The final part of the process is implementing the programmes in an effective way and budgeting for performance variations. The principles of human motivation are universal. We will explore programmes from around the world to show that subject to cultural attitudes the rules for sound employee motivation can be applied wherever you happen to be based. By the end of this review you should be able to improve the operational effectiveness of your current schemes, create new ones with confidence and have a broader understanding of why reward and recognition programmes are designed the way they are and how to make them more effective when the opportunity comes to review how they operate.

There is often a specific issue with non-monetary rewards, better described as incentives, which are over and above take-home pay and benefits. Daniel Pink, in *Drive* (2009), describes the phenomenon very succinctly: 'Goals may cause systematic problems for organizations due to narrowed focus, unethical behaviour, increased risk-taking, decreased cooperation and decreased intrinsic motivation.'

So, before you know it, you have a dozen reward and recognition (R&R) programmes running, none of which are 'working'. The larger the organization, the worse the cumulative effect is. Every three or four years, a new VP or senior executive comes in and decides to review it all. The same analysis of performance is undertaken with the same sample groups of workers. A new scheme is born, using new research to support the changes in emphasis. This may be about reward choice, team structures, new recognition media or possibly issues to do with the communication media or even the underlying economy itself. But they don't work either – or, at least, not as well as the return on investment (ROI) proposal said they would. ROI is the standard measure most programmes are subject to in order to determine what organizational benefit may derive from implementing them. But it is hard to establish such a measure for employee schemes, as sponsors often say that administration teams are almost impossible to measure in terms of returns in the financial sense. It would appear that changing human performance at work is not as easy as it looks.

A recent white paper by one of the world's leading 'performance improvement' consultancies, BI Inc, supported by many other earlier studies, declared that gift cards with a monetary value, for example, are less effective than tangible items such as merchandise in promoting higher performance – and yet most large multinationals still use gift cards or other cash substitutes as the go-to reward for employee incentives, recognition and reward.

Furthermore, the report says, gift cards actively encourage winners to add as much as 220 per cent of the reward in their own cash when they are redeeming. So most of the reward is, in fact, funded by the participants themselves, out of their own pockets. Was this really what was intended by the sponsor? What started out as a discretionary incentive and a reward for superior performance has become a discount on cash purchases employees may well have been planning to make anyway.

Incentives versus recognition

Then there's the idea that recognition is for employees and incentives are for salespeople, largely speaking. The accepted wisdom is that employees get recognition only because, to be frank, it is too expensive to give them all lavish rewards. On the other hand salespeople need incentives because they have little job security beyond achieving their targets. Just as with politicians, most salespeople's careers end in failure. Incentives compensate for the fact they will at some stage falter in their expected performance and be out of a job.

What is often not appreciated is that recognition and reward/incentives are part of the same continuum, with low-cost, esteem communication at one end and naked, somewhat expensive bribery, you might say, at the other. Recognition is usually long term. Incentives are usually short term. Recognition promotes loyalty, whereas incentives promote quick, tactical change. They are rarely mutually exclusive. Some of the best examples of incentives are in fact long-term recognition schemes for salespeople, such as sales clubs.

But few programmes are sufficiently well thought through to allow for both types of motivational intervention to take place. Why it tends to be one or the other remains a corporate, decision-making mystery. There should be no reward without recognition and no recognition without reward, even if it is only in token amounts of either element.

Does recognition really work?

If an employee goes above and beyond the call of duty and provides exceptional service or assists with an unexpected commercial deal many organizations will recognize this performance publicly and sometimes attach a small reward to say thanks. But why? Because they know that better employee engagement with the published values of the business leads to better bottom-line performance and in turn a higher stock price. But many managers need to be taught how to look out for exceptional performance and promote it appropriately. In some cultures singling out team members for specific praise is actually frowned upon. In some circumstances the praise itself may be demotivational for other team members, who may claim that the recognized person is not as hard-working as they are and that the boss never notices their efforts. Many managers say that identifying employees for special praise leads to more harm than good, as they cannot be expected to spot every incidence of exceptional performance. So the model of praising everyone for everything is not necessarily effective. It's all about context.

Who decides what level of reward is appropriate? Typically, administration staff receive much lower rewards than salespeople do for what might be described as similar exceptional activities. And is the size of the reward relevant anyway for employees who have an intrinsic interest in doing the tasks for the tasks' sake?

The balanced scorecard

One way around this dual tension is to introduce the balanced scorecard or a system based on key performance indicators (KPIs). In theory this provides a way to recognize and reward great all-round performance whether you administrate policy or you sell products. The trouble is, once the internal group of 'advisers' get their teeth into the constituents which make up good performance, things start to get complicated. Rather than, say, four components, most programmes end up with over a dozen measurements, which makes isolating what is essential for each individual virtually impossible. When you add the complexity of different job roles and the various operating divisions or global sites you begin to accumulate a highly complex, interlocking motivation programme that no one understands. The easiest solution for most employees is then simply to become non-combatants and sit this one out by withdrawing their willing participation.

Bribery and corruption

It is an unfortunate perception that for many organizations commercial incentives are viewed as being almost the same as bribery. Bribery and corruption are clearly an undesirable fact of commercial and organizational life. Where there is pressure to provide a profitable service to a large corporation there is the potential for corruption of the employed gatekeepers. In most of the industrialized West both offering and accepting personal gain in return for favouring a specific supplier is now a criminal rather than just a civil offence. Those involved could be imprisoned and the organization itself barred from future public sector tenders.

This was not always the case, and in many countries around the world either there is still no provision in law to combat commercial bribery or society itself turns a blind eye. It is simple to understand the moral argument of trying to create a level commercial playing field and punishing bribery. But some industry sectors such as pharmaceuticals and financial services have taken both an ethical and a legal stance to curb the worst excesses of trying to influence inappropriate selling. In the process this has led to an overzealous rejection of any kind of incentive, inducement or relationship building, even when it is perfectly justified to promote the organization's products. At what precise point do advertising, hospitality, special offers and sales promotion end and bribery begin? After all, isn't all marketing bribery of a kind?

The growing trend to equate gift cards with corruption and sports event tickets with bribery has redrawn the commercial landscape in recent years. Aviva, the UK insurance organization, declared in March 2014 that they would no longer entertain intermediaries at their various sponsored sporting events in the belief that this unfairly induced the intermediaries to place more business with the insurer.

It is perfectly acceptable for any organization to allocate their marketing allowance in the most effective way, of course. Many people suspect that this was more of a corporate cost-cutting measure than a moral stance, as it was convenient to reduce promotional expenditure during a downturn. But it sends a message that 'incentives' in any commercial context are not acceptable, even in the most benign circumstances. This attitude leads to less overall encouragement of employees within the workplace when it comes to reinforcing above-average performance. This is an unfortunate and unforeseen consequence of rejecting incentives as a common, effective motivational tool for managers.

Such changes in policy have meant that the very word 'incentive' has acquired a negative connotation, and organizations are beginning to reject the use of non-cash incentives, simply to avoid the potential accusation of being named as corrupt, such is the power of the media to make everyone and everything average and conformist.

As in life, there is a role for incentives in business if they are commercially effective and legal. It would be foolish of any policy maker to ignore the behavioural truths that show that offering incentive rewards produces benefits in performance. Incentives and recognition can be an untapped source for good in all organizations, provided they are offered in the right way with the right messages supporting them and in the right context.

The non-cash improvement dividend

The main reason for exploring what recognition and non-cash incentives can bring to any organization is to produce higher performance.

When you research employee groups about rewards, most people will say that more money at the end of the week or the month will motivate them to work harder. In fact, people actually work harder for non-cash items and tangibles (consumer goods and merchandise). So it is in the organization's interests and those of the stockholders to promote non-cash rather than cash solutions when devising motivation schemes.

Mazda Motor of America Inc

For instance, let us take a look at a programme for Mazda Motor of America Inc. This is a classic case history from 1996 whenever organizations are debating incentive programmes to encourage higher sales.

The marketing team were tasked with devising the next sales incentive to boost quarterly sales of its B-Series trucks within its North American operation of 900 Mazda car dealers. They had about 2,000 sales managers and 6,000 salespeople at the time. It was important to get the rewards right. It almost goes without saying that there would be a prestigious travel incentive for the top 15 dealers and their partners. In this case it turned out to be Aspen, Colorado. But what should be offered to the remaining sales managers and salespeople? The upper tier of sales management were edging towards a cash-per-sale solution, as this would be relatively easy to set up from a rewards administration viewpoint. But others lower down the hierarchy wanted a non-cash scheme, as they had experienced the effect of tangible rewards rather than extra money and saw that non-monetary rewards were much more effective in 'moving the metal'. There was no agreement.

It was decided that they would test the alternatives by splitting the dealer group in half, reminiscent of the King Solomon story from the Bible. Individual salespeople in group 1 would be offered an average of $75 in cash. Those in group 2 would be offered the same value in household merchandise and gift cards. There was a chance of earning more than $75 for a unit sale with a random win element called 'spin and win' – a common device to help promote the programme to incentive-aware showroom salespeople. The difference in cost to the organization was minimal.

The results were remarkable. Even experienced VPs had to admit that non-cash was more effective. The cash group only managed a 2.13

per cent uplift in sales. The non-cash group achieved a 15.65 per cent increase. In particular, sales performance amongst the hard-to-impress low-volume dealers in the non-cash group was very strong.

The post-programme analysis revealed that the perception of the cash incentive, particularly amongst low-volume dealers, was that the amounts after deductions for tax were marginal and there was little enthusiasm for what was in basic terms a mathematical deal. The non-cash dealers became fully engaged in identifying specific items of merchandise and retail gifts and organized their sales routines around achieving specific objectives to qualify for the rewards. It generated an emotional response rarely seen with cash-only programmes within commercial environments.

Some definitions

Before we go much further it is worth being clear about what we mean by rewards, incentives and recognition.

In this book rewards mean tangible, non-monetary items that participants receive in a motivation programme. So we are not talking about cash, salary, stock options or the range of benefits that employment brings with it in many organizations. Such items form part of the total remuneration package that compensates employees for their time and expertise at work. These benefits or perks do not promote higher performance, as we shall learn in Chapter 1.

Incentives, rather than incentive rewards, refer to the entire programme of activity that encourages participants to go above and beyond standard levels of work achievement. In many instances it is something that happens in the future. Once the programme is over the 'prizes' are then referred to as the rewards. It is true that commentators often use the terms 'reward' and 'incentive' to mean the same thing to describe the benefit the participant receives for compliance. So we have to be forgiving and accept that not everyone shares the same view of these definitions.

Recognition is a formal programme of congratulation for going beyond the call of duty and achieving something exceptional as measured by your organization's values. It does not necessarily include rewards, but it could do. The Human Capital Institute, amongst others, defined recognition as: 'Acknowledging or giving special attention to employee actions, efforts, behaviour or performance' (2009). It specifically refers to the employer recognizing employees rather than acknowledging distributor performance.

When we discuss reward and recognition programmes there is often an element of cost involved. To avoid the confusion of exchange rates between currencies the cost figures in the book have no currency denomination. This makes calculations easier to understand.

Where to start?

If you are sincere about wanting to improve employee and business partner performance, you need a plan or strategy. In short, a strategy is a list of four or five things that you intend to do differently to gain a competitive edge. Strategies are easy to come up with if you have a completely new product in a new sector. But the vast majority of business ideas are 'me-too' organizations where success depends on doing things in a new or unexpected way in comparison with your competitors. Even if the strategy is price-driven there comes a point when all organizations with price as their only strategy will begin to lose money. You have to have a plan.

So organizations search for a differentiator that will help them be more attractive to consumers than a seemingly similar rival. That differentiator is normally related to their employee profile. That people difference is a direct reflection of their internal reward and recognition programmes.

Brand consistency

Reward and recognition programmes need to reflect fully the organization's brand. Brand is an expression of buyer trust at its most basic level. If your core values are clear to the customer, your internal programmes should be consistent with those values as well. There is nothing more off-putting than a public angel that conceals a private devil.

To claim the reward and recognition dividend, employees need to be treated like customers and communicated with in a brand-consistent way. Loyalty reduces recruiting costs and requires the employer to train fewer people than its competitors. If employees know their corporate values they do not need to waste time asking what they should do when it comes to decision making.

Performance improvement model

The basis of all programmes is sound psychological theory that supports the idea that modern, non-monetary reward and recognition schemes have a solid and relatively predictable basis. Otherwise we are building our programmes on shifting sand. If what we do reflects what real humans do, we are probably on to a good thing. The process we should undertake when planning all R&R programmes is known as the performance improvement model. There are four steps:

1 We need to do some research to understand what is different about our own organization before imposing another new programme on unsuspecting employees. Part of this research is to establish an ROI for the activity. No organization would embark on an advertising campaign without working out the commercial benefit. Your people programmes are no exception to good business practice.

2 People do not change their behaviour without understanding the need for change and the consequences of not changing. So there is a place for skills development within the performance improvement model.

3 We should then take a close look at the incentive media or rewards and learn how to apply them and budget for them for the various employee audiences we have.

4 Probably most important of all is devising the communication plan. Post-programme surveys almost always reveal that most participants did not understand what they had to do or did not take part because they could not work out the scheme rules.

There are also some specific guidelines when it comes to running campaigns in more than one country. The mechanical issues of different currencies and delivering rewards pale into insignificance when thinking about cultural differences and how you might create a global scheme that suits all your locally sited employees, if you are an international firm. Problems in implementing such programmes are dealt with in Chapter 12.

Strategic employee incentives and recognition programmes are all about creating a framework for tapping into the extra potential for exceptional human effort at work. In the process of devising and running an effective programme you will be making work more engaging for the people who spend most of their working lives thinking about their team leaders and the organizational style of their workplace, whether they mean to or not.

John Fisher, Oxford, 2015
John.fisher@fmigroup.co.uk

Why 'benefits' do not deliver performance improvement

01

Before we start to think about non-monetary reward and recognizing achievement, we need to slay a few motivational dragons. In this chapter we will discuss the role that benefits or perks play in the remuneration of employees and why, in general, they do not tend to promote better performance.

Benefits such as free healthcare, childcare subsidies or perks such as access to discounted employee lunches or local gym membership are certainly valuable parts of any remuneration package and can, in some personal circumstances, make employees stay longer or even decide in their absence to resign and join someone new. But let's be clear. They do not improve individual performance at work or reinforce achievement habits.

Employee benefits and perks are neither recognition nor reward, despite their huge presence in the organizations of the developed world. It has been estimated that benefits account for 30 per cent or more of total employee costs for many large organizations. The concept of employee support benefits in the industrialized West originated in the 19th century in the UK to encourage people living in rural areas to move to the growing urban populations. Entire villages and communities were constructed by employers such as Cadbury and other Quaker employers as part of their Christian duty to care for their workers.

Society has moved on since those pioneering days, but benefits have remained a significant part of the competitive employment offer in most industrialized nations. With many employees enjoying lifestyles well above the poverty line in the developed world, benefits have become part of the incentive to attract new employees and retain the ones you already have. According to the Chartered Institute for Personnel and Development, some 90 per cent of UK employees now receive benefits and perks of one kind or another as part of their remuneration package.

Mattel, the toy manufacturer, offers some of its workers 16 hours of paid leave a year for parent- or school-related activity. Deloitte, the management consultancy, provides a sabbatical of three to six years of part-paid leave to pursue approved life- or career-enhancing activities. 3M offers time with 'mentor mums' to pregnant employees to help with the challenge of starting a family.

In the United States, 'fringe benefits' came into their own after the Second World War when there was a government freeze on wages by the War Labor Board. Employers sought other ways to make their organizations more attractive to would-be employees, despite the general levels of post-war austerity, and began to add benefits to their employment offer.

Tax treatment of benefits and perks

Health insurance as provided by employers in the United States was taxable prior to 1954, but it now stands outside the tax regime. Fiscal treatment of specific benefits is always subject to change depending on the policy makers in power. Every tax jurisdiction has various allowances and tax-exempt procedures for benefits and perks that make the specific item either more or less attractive for recipients.

It could be argued that the rise of the internet for exchange of business information in the late 1990s also accelerated the use of remuneration that stands outside the published salary scales. As almost any service or item of merchandise can now be offered at a discount and paid for electronically there is virtually no limit to the number and types of perk that workers can be offered. Savings can be much more pronounced online depending on the type of supplier, and the more employees you have the more likely the discount will be substantial.

But benefits or perks should not be confused with 'incentives'. When employee motivation is discussed at C-suite level, VPs often say that, if employees are not motivated to work harder with all the benefits they currently receive, why should the organization be offering similar non-monetary rewards for them simply to do their contracted job? This type of analysis misunderstands employee motivation at its most basic level. Nobody works harder or goes the extra mile for an increment in their pension or for higher life insurance.

Benefits exist to retain staff and promote loyalty. They do not encourage higher or exceptional performance on a day-to-day basis. Nor are they designed to do so. When you review the exit surveys of workers who have voluntarily left their jobs, very few leave because their 'perks and benefits' were not good enough. Most leave because they do not get on with their direct line supervisor or manager. When it comes to employee motivation there are bigger issues at stake when deciding to stay with an organization than childcare subsidies and retirement planning. The main reason can be found in Herzberg's seminal study about satisfiers and dissatisfiers, which was originally undertaken during the 1950s and continued throughout his professional life until his death in 2000.

The Motivation to Work by Frederick Herzberg (1959)

The original study was pretty small by the modern standards of 'big data' analysis. Herzberg, along with various research colleagues, analysed the responses to a survey of some 200 engineers and accountants in the Pittsburgh district. Rather than use closed questions requiring a yes/no answer or multiple choice options Herzberg asked open-ended questions about attitudes to incidents at work.

He cross-referenced his survey across some 150 other similar studies that had been undertaken since the 1920s, which provided a unique insight into the interpretation and grouping of the answers. Herzberg's theory attempts to show that to improve performance at work you should provide 'satisfiers'. Simply removing 'dissatisfiers' will not be effective, even though it would appear it should. This is the crux of the whole argument about whether perks and work benefits are there to improve performance or are there for some other reason.

Let's take a look at what Herzberg's diagram (Figure 1.1) actually means. There is an upright scale on the left-hand side which goes from 50 per cent dissatisfaction at the top down to 50 per cent satisfaction. If you are at 0 per cent the factor is neither a satisfier nor a dissatisfier, in theory. The first six grey bars reading left to right are the main factors that the 200 people in Pittsburgh mentioned as providing the most satisfaction at work. We can see this because the bars stretch way down into the 'satisfier' zone. In order, they are a sense of achievement, personal or team recognition, the intrinsic value of the work itself, role responsibility, the opportunity to be promoted (advancement) and personal growth in terms of learning something new. These are known as the 'motivator factors'. The implication is that if you want to motivate workers to make incremental effort or be more fully engaged or more committed to their job roles the

FIGURE 1.1 Herzberg's two-factor theory

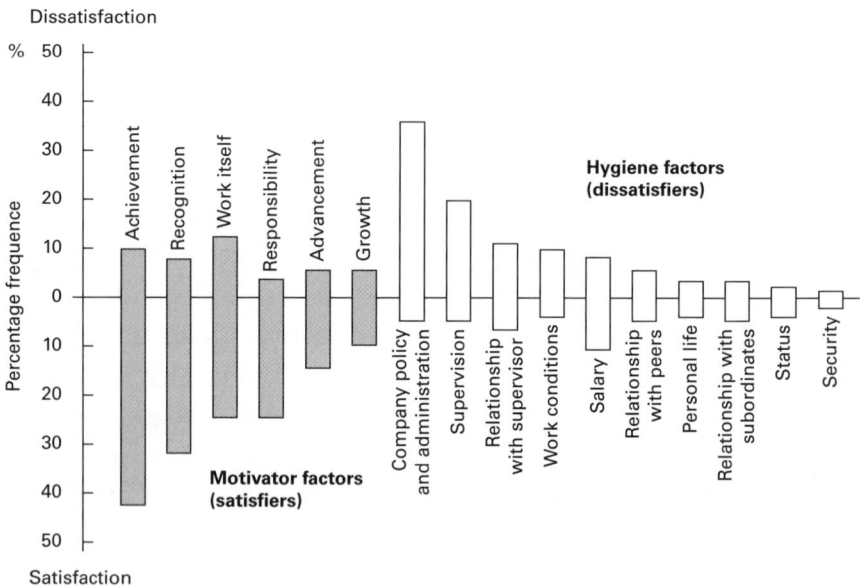

organization needs to build processes and programmes that allow these factors to flourish. So to promote higher performance and productivity management should concentrate on developing the 'motivator' factors.

On the right-hand side of Figure 1.1 are the hygiene factors, or the dissatisfiers. In other words, they represent all the factors that make workers dissatisfied with their job role. There may be other factors in any given organization that make people dissatisfied with their work situation, but in this study these were the factors that the respondents highlighted. Reading from left to right the factor most likely to cause dissatisfaction is company policy and administration. We then have supervision (or you could say the personal style of management prevalent in the organization), interpersonal relationships with immediate bosses or supervisors, work conditions, salary (which would include any perks or benefits), relationships with peers, personal life issues, relationship with subordinates, status within the organization (such as job title or inclusion within certain project teams) and lastly security (which points to the financial viability or stability of the organization in general). It is clear from the length of the bars (number of incidents recorded in the original survey) that company management style and the way you are personally managed are by far the biggest dissatisfier factors. In almost every employee survey since this survey was undertaken management style is quoted as the crucial factor in staff retention. The other factors are fairly neutral, as they cluster mostly around the zero axis.

Only 'motivators' improve work performance

What does all this mean with regard to reward and recognition? It strongly suggests that, if they want to improve workers' performance, organizations should spend most of their time on programmes that provide focus on individual achievement, recognition and incentives based on agreed performance goals rather than adjusting salary and benefits levels and all the other hygiene factors, which are mostly neutral in their effect according to Herzberg's diagram (Figure 1.1).

It would be useful for any organization to survey what total worker hours are spent internally on organizing the hygiene factors and what worker hours are dedicated to creating motivator factors. I suspect the time would be heavily skewed towards the dissatisfiers, even though we already know that the satisfiers are actually what make people improve their daily performance.

Naturally, no single activity carried out by the organization has just one effect. It can be argued that providing competitive benefits packages adds to the bottom line of quarterly figures because better retention equals reduced recruitment and training costs. It may also reduce the amount of time employees spend being disengaged and seeking other employment when they should be working on organizational tasks. But these positives are difficult to track and not scientifically verifiable.

One note of caution is the usual one of proportion and timing. It would be simply wrong to look at organizational planning out of context regarding the marketplace and the competitive environment. If a new competitor opened up on your doorstep and was paying 20 per cent higher salaries for the same job roles, you would certainly need to look at remuneration policy quickly rather than embark solely on a recognition programme and ignore the benefits package. All organizations work within a local competitive or sector framework, which is constantly changing. Simply following Herzberg's principles to the exclusion of all others would be foolish. But the evidence shows that only programmes that promote motivators produce higher performance at work. Benefits are the least effective use of resources and budget to encourage higher performance.

Does Herzberg's theory suggest more use of incentives?

It is clear from Figure 1.1 that anything that fosters the celebration of individual achievement and its communication throughout the organization can only be a force for good, all other things being equal. This leads on logically to providing incentives or contingency-based rewards to bring out that innate yearning for achievement and to setting up communication programmes to promote team and individual recognition of those 'achievements'.

Cash or non-cash?

The big debate then moves on to whether the incentives should be money or some other type of reward. According to the Herzberg model, more money (or extra salary) is a hygiene factor and so is not a medium to help improve performance. But we know that commission schemes and bonuses do work in some way to promote higher activity, so shouldn't they be a 'motivator'? (For the answer see Chapter 8.) The broad answer is that surprisingly most people do not work harder for 'more money'. In fact in many knowledge-based organizations, which includes most jobs in the developed world, the work itself is the main driver of high performance, and purely adding more money can actually impair performance and cause friction between employees, leading to lower individual performance, not higher achievement.

We should say something about motivation programmes in general and why they exist. Professional managers with hands-on experience of one-to-one management of individuals and teams will often say that they do not need such techniques to create additional performance. This is no doubt true for many. But what about those who are new to the management of incentive and recognition programmes or simply do not have the communication skills to pull them off in an effective way? According to the 'span of seven' rule, any group larger than seven needs to be motivated remotely in some shape or form. Humans find it difficult to manage personally each individual beyond this number. The role of a centrally organized programme is to ensure that there is a professional framework around which even an averagely competent manager can work.

Sometimes line supervisors complain that the catch-all programme does not work for them within the context of their team or their division. Any general programme introduced for the entire organization for something as personal as individual recognition and reward is probably going to be valid for only say 80 per cent of any given audience. But this is not a reason to abandon the attempt. Organizational life is full of instances where policy or processes are only ever partially achieved. The objective is to achieve as high an uptake as possible, provide remedies for those areas that do not participate and accept the rest as the statistical tail of non-compliance. This is what engagement is all about.

A further issue may be that the programme as devised by the central team has the wrong key performance indicators (KPIs) for their specific division or has a theme that does not resonate with their operational processes. This can be most often experienced by employees who work in advice areas such as consultancy, legal or senior management. Hybrids of the overall programme can easily be produced that offer a similar focus on recognition and incentives but that are relevant to the procedures of a particular area. It simply requires some imagination to see how to dovetail the main programme into more specialized parts of the organization.

Are there any other motivational theories to consider?

Herzberg is quite clear when it comes to isolating what factors would promote better employee performance, but unfortunately not all academic researchers are such good communicators. Often behavioural patterns observed in lab rats are used to illustrate the power of offering incentives. But do the findings apply to humans? Numerous studies over the years have been conducted using students, as they are a cheap and convenient source of compliant survey fodder. But do they really represent how employed workers or professionals would behave in the context of a busy working day?

There is no doubt that theories can point to a number of operational guidelines for programme planners from how often to send messages to the type of reward to offer. They are all top-line findings and may or may not apply to every single organizational situation, but they do answer some of the detailed queries that often come up when the planning for reward and recognition programmes gets under way.

Benefits and perks are not the answer

It is clear from this chapter that although benefits and perks are widely used across the developed world to attract and retain employees they do a very poor job when it comes to encouraging higher performance. The main issue is that they are not contingent on any kind of behaviour, but are an entitlement of being employed. Despite their aggregate cost they are far from transparent in terms of their effectiveness in promoting a more achievement-driven, results-based workforce.

If we now agree that programmes to promote achievement and recognition are the most effective way to improve individual worker and team performance, we need to think about incentive or human motivation theory a little more before we start constructing a strategic reward and recognition plan for any organization. Knowing something specific about human behaviour could save you a lot of money, if the knowledge is applied correctly and in context, especially if large numbers of people are involved.

Recognition and reward theory

02

If we want to be strategic about rewards (non-monetary incentives) we need to know what works and what does not. As any business consultant will tell you, every organizational situation is different. But surely there must be some motivational principles on which you can base your programmes? The issue with human motivation theory is that we are all experts, perhaps, and all have direct experience of being motivated and demotivated by the actions of others in the workplace. Because of this collective wisdom there will be no shortage of peers, bosses and team members ready to tell you what works and what does not. A more effective way to take advice about reward and recognition programmes is to look at some of the main theories of human behaviour and see if any of those have a direct relevance to employee performance. Indisputable truths can also help you to avoid the more obvious and expensive errors.

Thinking about human motivation has always been with us. Since the days of Ancient Greece, when philosophers such as Democritus and Epicurus first outlined the principles of hedonism, the idea that humans are motivated by their desires to behave in a particular way has attracted many theories. William James (1890) encapsulated pre-modern-age attitudes to human motivation with the following statement in his *Principles of Psychology*: 'But as present pleasures are tremendous reinforcers, and present pains tremendous inhibitors of whatever action leads to them, so the thoughts of pleasures and pains take rank amongst the thoughts which have most impulsive and intuitive power.' The doctrine of hedonism has much to recommend it as a way to approach employee motivation for positive engagement. Epicurus' main idea was that the greatest good (the recommended approach to life) would come from modest, 'sustainable' pleasure in the form of tranquillity, freedom from fear and the absence of bodily pain. Unlike the modern perceived meanings of hedonism, the original idea was to aim for having no desires at all or as few as possible, as this leads ultimately to happiness. Many people will recognize this idea as the main thrust behind Buddhism.

Although we can observe every day how the pleasure-versus-pain principle explains much about why people behave in a certain way in any given situation it is not particularly helpful when trying to improve business performance. We need to predict what employees will *actually* do in practice. The idea of any organization in the 21st century deliberately organizing internal processes to inflict physical or mental pain on employees is unlikely to gain much traction, but the principle of making the working environment more pleasurable and less painful so as to attract and retain employees is certainly the basis of many modern well-being programmes.

The concept of tranquillity is also useful in designing organizational processes to reduce friction and conflict between working groups in any joint enterprise. But these principles are very broad in nature and not scientifically predictive. What modern organizations require is to make the ROI case to spend discretionary budget on managed programmes that will contribute to the bottom line.

The ancient thinkers were applying their minds to life in general for a relatively elite group of people who, in the main, did not have to earn to survive or work in groups, the military excepted. They certainly had no commercial benefit in mind. It was not until the late 19th and early 20th centuries that thinkers turned their attention to how large groups of people in a common enterprise behave so as to provide advice to governments, institutions and commercial organizations about how to improve overall efficiencies. As soon as there was a cost imperative to finding the answer – better use of taxpayers' funds, more efficient spending of charitable donations, or better investment of shareholders' contributions – the search for some guiding principles for human motivation at work within an organizational framework became more urgent. Reducing waste and being more efficient have no doubt raised the need to motivate people better at work, but what motivates workers to perform better even if they are already contracted to do the job has become a key issue for many organizations.

What drives employees to perform better?

What exactly should owners or managers be doing to encourage higher performance other than removing physical pain and improving whatever pleasure there may have been in the processes of work and the working environment? During the 20th century many psychologists and social scientists conducted numerous experiments within factory or enterprise environments to determine what made employees work more efficiently. Initially there was an emphasis on improving productivity through the mechanistic processes of Taylor (2014) and then to such experiments as Elton Mayo's well-documented Hawthorne findings (2010) to see if changes to the environment made a difference to productivity. Later researchers moved on to the psychological aspects of behaviour to appeal to the way workers were treated rather than just their physical capacity to 'work harder'. Interaction and better group work turned out to be part of the answer for improving performance.

Experimental timeline

Martin Ford's (1992) *Motivating Humans* draws up a timeline for all the major human motivation theories since the early 20th century, and from them we can see the direction of travel in modern, work-related thinking. Not all the theories relate directly to working processes, so I have included just those that seem to have something useful to say about motivating people at work. Although Table 2.1 stops at 1992, this should not suggest that no further ideas have been produced since then: far from it. The truth is that basic concepts do not come

TABLE 2.1 Human motivation theories timeline

	Topic	Author	Title
1901	Psychoanalytic theory	Freud	The pleasure principle
1911	Scientific management	Taylor	Efficiency is everything
1933	Human relations	Mayo	Worker interaction
1938	Psychogenic needs	Murray	20 basic human needs
1943	Hierarchy of needs	Maslow	Satisfying needs gradually
1943	Drive theory	Hull	Physiological drive elements
1953	Achievement	McClelland	Predicting effort from incentive
1964	Job satisfaction	Vroom	Work choices and performance
1966	Two-factor theory	Herzberg	Hygiene versus motivators
1968	Goal setting	Locke and Latham	Feedback on goals
1968	Social facilitation	Cottrell	Improving group tasks
1975	Optimal experience	Csikszentmihalyi	Flow and satisfaction
1990	Goals and performance	Latham *et al*	Performance management
1992	Human motivation	Ford	Motivation systems theory

along every year, and many are evolving based on older ideas. As a starting point Table 2.1 covers the main strands of research and thought that can be of some practical use when it comes to planning effective organizational motivation programmes.

From the selective timeline in Table 2.1 it can be seen that the initial interest in human motivation for its own sake quickly gave way to how any predictive findings could be used for organizational or commercial benefit. Frederick Taylor was one of the first to begin analysing the question as to whether employees would work harder if they were offered incentives such as more money. The results formed the basis of many piece-work or commission schemes that are still in use today. He founded the scientific management movement, which broadly set out to simplify work processes and pay employees for better productivity of simple tasks. In time he developed changes in equipment and working practices to get the most efficient result. His four basic principles were:

- Use *measurement* and scientific analysis to determine the best way to complete any task.
- *Assign* workers who showed specific aptitude to a specific task.
- Measure *performance* and allow supervisors to manage performance actively.
- *Split management or training tasks* from pure production to ensure the best (most efficient) use of resources.

Many of these ideas seem like common sense today. There is still much to be said for designing the right tools for the right job to get the best result. In addition, recruiting employees with an appropriate set of skills was by no means the obvious thing to do pre-Taylor, and he can be credited with a primary role in preparing the way for modern recruitment and training methods.

The major criticism of Taylor's approach remains that not all people are the same and that working as a team or simply for the intrinsic enjoyment of the task itself can be more productive than mechanically going through the processes laid down by others for workers without any discussion. Taylor was also somewhat simplistic in his approach to incentives in that money was the only incentive he believed in. This may have been self-evident when times were hard and consumer choice was limited, but as we shall see later, in the developed world of the 20th century more money can actually impair rather than enhance performance if employees are not working simply to exist. Recognition can go a long way in the overall motivation of employees in the modern world and may even be more effective than reward in improving productivity.

The rise of teamwork and affiliation

It was Elton Mayo in the 1920s who first suggested that the preconceptions of scientific management were not delivering the results many people expected they would in the world of work. Mayo's experiments into the effect of changing working conditions took place between 1924 and 1933 in the Bell System's Western Electric Company in Hawthorne, near Chicago. The purpose of the experiments was to endorse Taylor's scientific approach, but they uncovered a completely new 'truth' when it came to worker performance – that environmental factors may not be as important as first thought. Perhaps better performance lay in the interaction between workers and their supervisors rather than purely people's work conditions. The results or rather the interpretation of the data led to much speculation about what they *actually* proved. The discussion amongst social scientists continues to this day.

In simple terms the research team wanted to show the effects on output productivity of changing factors in the work environment, such as lighting levels, work pauses, incentive pay and work autonomy. The statistical results showed that any changes in productivity were not significantly affected by changes in work conditions – unless they were extreme, such as very low lighting levels. Higher productivity came from increased social interactivity and to some extent the special status workers enjoyed from being the subject of experimental research. Attempts were made to cancel out this effect by subtle or unannounced changes of conditions. But overall the conclusion was that giving autonomy to the working group and monitoring/supervising their performance and paying attention to their achievements produced higher performance.

The ironic conclusion therefore of the Hawthorne experiments was that teamwork and focus on performance are more important determinants of performance than small changes in hygiene factors such as lighting, work breaks and money incentives.

Basic physiological human needs

Having laid out the principles of scientific management when applied to groups, many researchers then turned their attention to the individual and whether there was something intrinsic about individual human behaviour at work that organizations could tap into to promote higher performance and better efficiency. Clark Hull in the 1940s started to look at 'drive' as being the determining factor as to why people do the things they do.

In 1943 he published *Principles of Behavior* in which he describes the idea that 'drive' is responsible for changes in behaviour and by isolating individual drives we can influence human behaviour. Everyone tends towards the status quo and strives to maintain it, interrupted from time to time by such factors as hunger, thirst and temperature. By satisfying these disruptions at the physiological level we can influence human behaviour in a predictive way. The satisfying of these needs then becomes reinforcement of behaviour. We are able to partially control human behaviour by providing or withholding specific drive satisfiers.

The value of Hull's experimentation was more in the method than the findings themselves. He established many ways to measure human behaviour in the presence or absence of specific factors, which assisted other researchers to look more closely at not just the physiological needs of humans but their social and psychological needs as well. Commercially, what organizations wanted to know was what made real people tick and how that latent capacity to perform better could be tapped into and used for the good of the organization.

Murray's basic human needs

At around the same time, Henry Murray (1938) declared there were, apparently, 20 basic psychological human needs, which he called 'psychogenic'. If these needs could be isolated, Murray argued, behaviour could be changed by sponsors or experimenters by playing on these needs to their possible advantage.

The psychogenic needs are worth exploring, as they say much about human behaviour at work. They are categorized into five types:

- *Ambition needs:*
  - achievement: the intrinsic reason why many professionals continue to strive to perform, even in the absence of any external incentives or direction;
  - exhibition: being shocking or getting reactions from others;
  - recognition: linked to achievement in the sense of striving for social status.

- *Materialistic needs:*
  - acquisition: at the time, this partially explained the consumer boom within the industrialized nations;
  - construction: being creative and making things or inventing processes;
  - order: administrating and organizing tasks;
  - retention: never throwing anything away, linked to acquisition.

- *Power needs:*
  - abasement: apologizing, admitting to mistakes;
  - autonomy: independence of thought and action;
  - aggression: attacking others, physically or verbally;
  - blame avoidance: following the 'rules';
  - deference: bowing to social pressure;
  - dominance: controlling other people.

- *Affection needs:*
  - affiliation: spending time socially with people;
  - nurturance: looking after others;
  - play: having 'fun';
  - rejection: the opposite of affiliation;
  - succour: being helped by others.
- *Information needs:*
  - cognizance: seeking knowledge;
  - exposition: educating others.

From this list of needs it is clear that each specific need could be the basis of a job specification for a defined role. If the person applying for the job exhibits high affiliation needs, that person is unlikely to be happy working alone with little interaction. Someone with low levels of cognizance applying to be a researcher is going to find the job difficult.

Taking a wider view, it could be argued that each person, if tested against a standard database, will have varying degrees of need and no single abnormality will rule the person out of a specific job role. Murray acknowledges that environment does play a part in human behaviour. For modern managers, simply being aware that most people have five basic types of need and so their performance at work can be partially explained (rather than predicted) by reference to them is a useful primer. Some leeway could therefore be given for the work group 'clown' or the 'blame avoider', and a clue provided as to how to manage such a person better going forward now that you know what that person's main need is.

Maslow's hierarchy of needs

During the 1940s there was a research scramble to come up with an all-encompassing explanation for human motivation and behaviour. Arguably the best-known and most quoted model for individual and indeed group behaviour was Maslow's hierarchy of

FIGURE 2.1 Maslow's hierarchy of needs

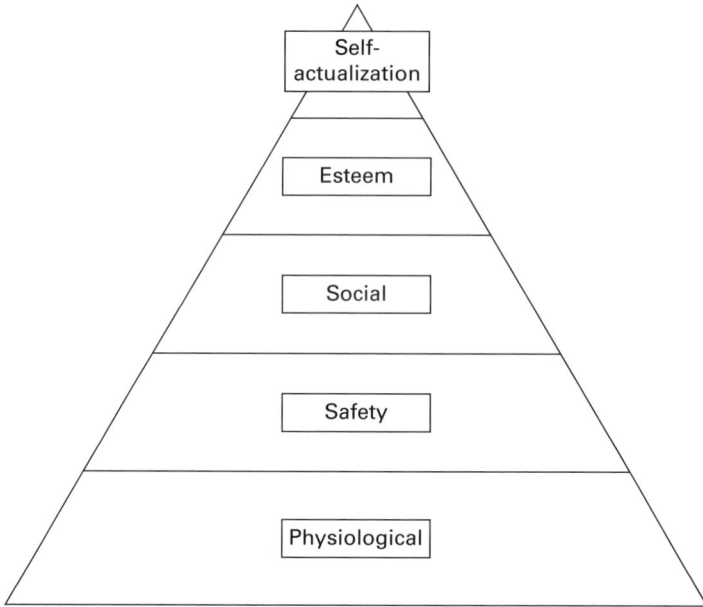

needs (Figure 2.1). To this day it remains one of the most useful concepts any supervisor can have to motivate individuals and groups better and with more predictive quality than broad ideas of need or human drives.

In 1943 Maslow published a paper called 'A theory of human motivation'. It proposed that there is a pecking order of motivational needs, which can be seen as a progressive scale, moving from the physiological to the quasi-spiritual. There are five needs. The lower need has to be satisfied before the next level of need can be satisfied.

For example, *physiological* needs come first. Someone without food or water is unlikely to be motivated by a prestige car or a new job role until that person's basic needs for physical survival have been met. The next level of need is *security* in the widest possible sense. This might include shelter, somewhere to live, job security and healthcare of some kind. The third need is for *social interaction*, not dissimilar to Murray's idea of 'affiliation'. This is a deep-seated need to belong to a group, whether social, religious or political – a sense of belonging. The fourth level of need is *esteem* or recognition of personal worth. This manifests itself in the need to be appreciated by peers and to excel in a particular skill that is valued by the group. The top level is *self-actualization*. In Maslow's world this means being interested in one's own personal growth or ambition and less concerned with the opinions of the social group. In concrete terms this could apply to a sportsperson, a career politician, a priest, an academic or an artist. Maslow describes this as follows:

> What a man *can* be, he *must* be. This need we may call self-actualization… It refers to the desire for self-fulfillment, namely, to the tendency for him to become actualized in what he is potentially. This tendency might be phrased as the desire to become more and more what one is, to become everything that one is capable of becoming.

Although the hierarchy looks fixed and rigid, this is not supported by later research, and even Maslow himself admitted that for some people social acceptance was more important than say self-actualization. In addition, these needs are not constant and can change over time. But the value of the concept is that it gives managers in organizations the vocabulary and opportunity to recognize deep-seated needs in individuals in the workplace. By recognizing that an individual is largely driven by a particular need the manager can then satisfy that need in order to promote higher performance.

Such individual needs could also apply to groups, by analogy. Figure 2.1 could be amended to show how the five levels might apply to group behaviour. For example, in the context of a sales team Maslow's hierarchy could be a way to devise a non-cash incentive scheme. Are the basic needs of salary or commission being met, as otherwise an incentive scheme with non-cash rewards might fall on stony ground? Is the organization in good financial health and so providing 'security' for its employees? If not, should not that element be fixed first before introducing discretionary incentives? Within the structure of the incentive scheme, have we built in graded rewards for achievement so that participants can feel they are part of a special group or club to respond to affiliation needs? For the higher achievers is there room in the structure to recognize and reward exceptional performance – a gold level – to meet the need for esteem? At the higher levels are we accommodating the esteem needs of the very best? Will there be winners, and will they be recognized as such?

The only oddity in the pyramid is self-actualization. In sales team terms this could be interpreted as that small group of high achievers who say they are driven by the need to be the best that they can be and not influenced by incentive programmes. Their value to the sponsoring organization, though, is in using them as role models for those who are still at the esteem stage. They can be useful examples to hold up to other strivers and demonstrate perhaps what 'great salespeople' look like to others who are still on the journey towards self-actualization.

At the individual level of one-to-one motivation it can be seen that dealing with individuals' need to feel secure in their job role or paying them a living wage has to come before they will be excited by an incentive scheme. Once that need is satisfied the manager has to focus on esteem needs for recognition and deliberately consider ways to recognize superior performance. At the very top end self-actualized professional people tend to be motivated by the job itself, so the manager needs to think of ways to grow the job remit or involve experienced people in new organizational projects as a way to tap into their highest needs.

Victor Vroom and job satisfaction

By the 1960s many social scientists were well down the road to clarifying many motivational needs in the context of the workplace. Job roles and job satisfaction began to become an important issue as organizations began to count the cost of recruiting and retaining workers. In *Work and Motivation*, Vroom (1964) outlines his idea that expectancy of a positive outcome is what drives employees to higher performance. In other words they work harder if they genuinely believe that there will be a positive result at the end, which includes a need they want satisfied such as a promotion, more responsibility and more involvement. In this situation managers should therefore emphasize these 'rewards' rather than just the promise of higher pay. This is evidenced by exit interviews of unsatisfied workers who say they were frustrated by working harder for less 'reward', which in their case was a feeling of job satisfaction and positive reinforcement.

One anecdotal aspect is the finding that offering high levels of monetary reward can actually be a deterrent to raising performance as the stress to over-perform then impairs the very performance you want to encourage. For some people the opportunity to earn great rewards seems to have the same effect as a rabbit caught in the headlights ... once in the spotlight, they freeze an become unsure what to do next.

Herzberg: two-factor theory

We discussed Herzberg's research in Chapter 1 and why Herzberg 'proves' that benefits are not motivators for most people. It is worth returning to Herzberg in the wider discussion about human motivation at work. In 1966 there was something of a turning point in work-related research, even though the sample was very small and localized. Frederick Herzberg surveyed some 200 accountants and professional people in full-time employment. Arguably for the first time he was able to isolate factors that produced dissatisfaction and those that promoted performance improvement at work. The categorization of factors of employment into hygiene factors and motivators suggested that the way to improve performance at work was to spend resources on the motivators rather than the hygiene factors, other than to remain competitive in the local marketplace.

The implication for the reward and recognition of professionals of equating 'satisfaction' with, say, performance or engagement is fundamental. Herzberg's work strongly suggests that performance managers or policy setters should concentrate on the motivators, not the hygiene factors to improve worker performance. This means more time and effort should be given to organizing achievement-based incentives, recognition schemes and job progression planning than to employee benefits and work conditions. The argument is that higher satisfaction levels can be gained by introducing a recognition programme than by supplying ever higher employee benefits, which produce only marginal effects on job satisfaction.

Goal setting and the quest for higher performance

By the 1970s, once organizations had taken on board the implications of job satisfaction and what could be done to support this basic need, attention had turned to setting appropriate goals and the motivational effect of using incentives to improve performance at work, particularly non-monetary incentives. What has become common sense about setting organizational goals needed to be researched and tested. Latham and Locke (1990) looked into what was required for the optimum achievement of goals and what inhibited performance of these goals.

According to the vast body of work that was accomplished on goal theory, the findings can be mercifully reduced to a few key pointers:

- Goals must be accepted prior to their pursuit by the participants, so the clear implication is for goals to be discussed and agreed rather than imposed.
- Goals must be specific and capable of being understood by the participants.
- Goals must be perceived to be fair and attainable.
- Feedback on progress towards goals improves their attainment.

All these points have clear implications for organizations, whose business is to set goals and hopefully achieve them. Budget discussions should therefore be bottom-up rather than top-down, and activities to achieve those goals should be mutually agreed rather than imposed from above. In practice this is self-evident, as organizations need people to achieve goals. Simply plucking performance goals out of the air is not going to motivate employees to achieve them.

Participants need to understand completely what is required. Typically this applies to performance programmes in which a certain level of performance results in a specific reward or level of recognition. The rules of a sales incentive project need to state clearly when the incentive period begins, when it ends, what products are included or excluded, who is included, and in what circumstances, if any, the programme would be cancelled or downgraded for whatever commercial reason.

Goals need to be perceived as attainable and appropriate to the circumstances. As much as an organization would like to improve its levels of employee engagement, for example, the goal needs to be attainable in, say, 80 per cent not 20 per cent of cases. If the goals are not perceived to be achievable participants will withdraw their commitment and the programme will fail.

Feedback on performance towards goals improves their attainment. When it comes to the reporting of corporate numbers of employees' progress or even lack of it, this needs to be regularly communicated to the participants so that work groups can realign their behaviour to achieve the goals. This is equally true of managing individuals. Appraisal systems should be constructed in such a way that feedback on performance is given not just once a year in formal circumstances but more regularly on an ongoing basis.

Cottrell and teamwork

In 1968 Cottrell set out his ideas for 'social facilitation' (Guerin, 2009: 51) within a work context whose principles were used in the construction of a new type of manufacturing plant in Kalmar, Sweden for Volvo, which reinvented the idea of the production line in manufacturing to be a team task rather than a Taylorian individual, mechanistic task. Henry Ford's original model of a highly specific manufacturing process was replaced, following the new group theories of worker involvement and engagement, by processes based on social facilitation:

> The new plant was constructed with many separate rooms, each with a
> separate entrance and large windows to the world outside. Old union
> job classifications were abolished, along with the common practice at
> conventional plants of workers standing idly by while waiting for a
> fellow worker with the 'proper' classification to perform a narrowly
> specified task. Instead, all workers were treated as interchangeable,
> and each room was given to a *team* of 15 to 25 workers who were
> made jointly responsible for performing, in a specified time, a broadly

defined task, such as electric wiring, door assembly, fitting upholstery, or installing an exhaust system. In each room, there might be 60 different things to do to finish the assigned task, and workers were free to decide how to do it and who did what and when. (This also reduced the need for lower-level management, such as foremen.) Once the task was done, the semi-finished car would move on to the next team, being carried about the plant on computer-controlled trolleys.

(Adapted from Kohler, 1997: 278–79, 411–13)

A further finding was the predictive power of people working together. Cottrell found that 'When two or more people act together the intensity of their individual behaviour often increases' (quoted in Simmel, 1968). This chimes well with other modern management theories of work performance such as peer group pressure and peer influence.

Goals and goal setting

Goals and goal setting are now at the heart of most modern organizational plans. Locke and Latham researched many aspects of goal setting during their careers (see Latham, 2012). The general view was that setting a specific, numerical goal and providing regular feedback on that goal is the most effective way of achieving it. Goals that are not stretching are unlikely to motivate participants to work harder. Locke and Latham proposed five main principles in the effective setting of performance goals:

- *Clarity:* Is it obvious what the participant has to do and is there an agreed measure of successful attainment?
- *Challenge:* The goal has to be challenging enough to engage with, stretching but doable.
- *Commitment:* Participants need to have any goals discussed and agreed before the goals are implemented; otherwise there will be no commitment to achieve them.
- *Feedback:* Regular and accurate feedback on performance improves the commitment to the goals being set.

- *Task complexity:* If the task is complex, more time may be needed to complete it. Creating stress to achieve a complex goal may be counter-productive and actually impair performance.

The implications of goal theory are clear when it comes to devising an effective reward and recognition programme. If the plans for launch do not follow these five principles, the programme is unlikely to be successful.

Flow and job satisfaction

Csikszentmihalyi published his first thoughts about 'happiness' and the importance of 'flow' in 1975 (see Csikszentmihalyi, 2002). Over the next 15 to 20 years he wrote and researched extensively about the idea that motivating people well requires them to attain a state of flow where they are fully engaged in a task and using their innate skills to the maximum. He argued that happiness or satisfaction can be a learned experience and that, by following certain activities, 'flow' can be achieved on a regular basis. This, of course, is of great interest to organizations that constantly suffer from workers who are rarely fully engaged with the tasks of the organization. To achieve flow:

- people should have clear goals with regular feedback on performance;
- there should be a balance between skills and challenge;
- action and awareness of those actions should happen simultaneously;
- there should be no failure anxiety;
- the sense of time should disappear;
- the activity should become an end in itself.

Many of these phrases will be familiar from the previous history of human motivation theory. In the context of being a business tool for devising job specifications, flow is a very useful concept in improving performance at work. Possibly the most important aspect is the idea that it is acceptable to fail within the organizational framework. This is not always an easy thing to sanction when there is always financial pressure to perform profitably and efficiently.

Performance and HR

Latham and various collaborators continued their work on goal setting and helping HR establish some practical ground rules for promoting higher performance at work. Clearly much has been written and continues to be written to refine and redefine what is meant by motivation, drive, recognition, incentive and performance at work. As far as a settled appreciation of having a system for HR and marketing practitioners is concerned it is probably Martin Ford's review of all the previous theories published as *Motivating Humans* in 1992 that stands out as an accessible and practical plan.

Principles of human motivation

As a result of reviewing all the previous published theories of human motivation Martin Ford proposed 16 key theories that could be used to motivate humans for more optimal performance. For our purposes we could call this 'performance at work', whether for an administrative worker, a top salesperson or a key distributor.

These theories could be headlined using the following formula, which neatly encapsulates all the known work on what makes people work harder:

$$\frac{\text{Motivation (strength of drives)} \times \text{Skill (competence)} \times \text{Responsive environment}}{\text{Biology (physiology)}}$$

In this formula you can see that job achievement is a combination of the strength of drives that individuals show factored by their skill or competence in the role and a responsive organizational environment. These three elements should then be moderated by an individual's physiology – the individual's general health and strength. As we have seen, all of these variables can be affected by organizational policies. It can be seen that implementing formal programmes both at the macro level and at the supervisor level will result in higher performance, all other things being equal.

Principles of corporate motivation

So having constructed a guiding 'universal' theory of how to motivate individuals based on all the previous but specific research into human motivation – and by extension groups of workers – we can

TABLE 2.2 Principles of corporate motivation

Motivation systems theory (MST) principles	Suggested programme
Suggested programme	Motivate the entire individual, not just one skill
Motivational triumvirate	Goals, emotions and participant commitment
Responsive environment	Teamwork and interaction
Goal activation	All programmes need clear goals
Goal salience	Goals should be clear and obvious
Multiple goals	Better to have more than one goal
Goal alignment	Goal should be aligned, not in conflict
Flexible standards	Change plans if circumstances change
Optimal challenge	Challenging but doable goals
Direct evidence	Testimonials breed credibility
Reality	Check skills and a responsive environment
Emotional activation	Appeals to emotion are more motivating
'Just do it'	Get started, even if change is small
Incremental change	Small steps are better than no steps
Equifinality	Try alternative approaches, or mix it up
Human respect	Treat people with respect, not as ciphers

then consider what actual programmes we need to implement to create higher performance. Having reached the point of a series of principles (Table 2.2) when constructing the ideal motivation programme based on a review of all the current research into human motivation we are now ready to put these principles into practice. It is obvious that an all-singing, all-dancing R&R motivation programme that covered all 16 motivational principles on each occasion is unlikely to be successful. In addition you run the risk of over-intellectualizing the process. The key issue is to bear these principles in mind when the programme is being constructed and, where possible, include the findings of motivational research into your plan, if practical.

Key concepts in human motivation theory

It seems a disservice to reduce over 100 years of behavioural research into one short chapter and then to pick out the things that are obvious for use by organizations and discard the rest, but scientific research has always produced more than can be applied at the practical level. For would-be motivation managers the main findings for organizational use are:

- Programmes need to reflect a broad range of motivational needs within any group of people.
- Details need to be discussed with the participants beforehand.
- Individual recognition is a powerful incentive towards higher performance.
- Teamwork creates higher performance than individuals working on their own, except for simple tasks.
- Rewards work better if they are personal to the individual.
- Goals should be challenging but doable.
- Vary your approach, and build a flexible programme.

Theory is hard to apply in the absence of an overall, commercial or organizational issue to tackle. How are the theories applied in practical terms and what kinds of programmes are run that use these theories, either in part or in whole? Most importantly, what levels of performance improvement should you expect to see in a well-researched and properly funded performance improvement programme?

Motivation in practice

03

Business improvement, performance improvement and incentive programmes are all based on sound human motivation principles, which we discussed in Chapter 2. But what do they look like in practice, and how was the theory used to make the schemes more effective? Is the theory just 'nice to know about' or is it crucial in the creation of strategic reward and recognition programmes? Every enhancement to a programme involves cost, but how do you know if that additional expense will have positive outcomes in terms of actual performance in the workplace?

Humans are not robots. No single technique will deliver improvements from everyone at all times in all situations, but the balance of probabilities shows that following research findings will be much more effective than simply hoping for the best. The difference with applying research in motivating humans is that people often respond in unexpected ways – and with most workers you rarely get a second chance to amend a poorly thought-through motivation programme. They have long memories when it comes to organizational mistakes. You may not get another chance. People often remember what went wrong with previous schemes rather than what went right.

In this chapter we explore what real organizations are doing to get greater performance using rewards and recognition across many sectors and in many markets. The same principles crop up across the examples because the theory is true of all human behaviour. Motivation programmes were not needed in the pre-industrial revolution era, as poverty and coercion were strong enough reasons for employees to toe the line. With the advent of more enlightened social policies and workers' rights, management had to consider more accommodating ways to produce higher efficiencies and therefore better profits. For small groups and teams you are better advised to manage their performance on a one-to-one basis. Typically when your supervisory span is more than 25 you will need to start thinking about strategic reward and recognition, as you cannot possibly micromanage individual performance on a daily basis with such numbers of people.

There are broadly two types of programme: reward or incentive schemes, which are mostly intended to promote more sales; and recognition projects, which are usually aimed at employees. Sales incentives are usually straightforward in terms of guiding principles: 'do this–get that'. But they can suffer from short-term gains that fall away once the programme is finished. The rewards, usually non-monetary, are all-important and often need to be eye-catching to compete with other rival manufacturers' programmes and be 'aspirational' rather than ordinary.

Recognition schemes are usually based on established organizational values. They tend to be long term and much more aligned to the culture of the organization. Rewards for employees are generally of a lower level than those offered to salespeople and often of token value rather than the more lavish budgets afforded to sales programmes, which have larger product margins to play with.

But it all depends what type of reward you are offering. An Incentive Federation survey in 2014 found that the average budget per head on sales/distributor travel incentives in the United States was around $3,440, whereas the equivalent gift card travel spend for non-sales employees was $2,291 – a reduction of one-third. The absolute numbers are less important than the differential. Because most non-sales programmes use gift cards as the main reward mechanism the average spend per head is much lower. The differential in incremental reward value is probably still around a third higher for sales workers than for support workers across most sectors.

Most programmes are sales-related

In the commercial world most employees' experience of incentive or reward programmes is likely to be of a 'do this–get that' type of scheme or a contingency-based competition. In fact some 70 per cent or more of motivation programmes are revenue-related in some way.

Volvo Cars UK is a typical example. In the 1980s, at the height of an economic surge, Volvo was concerned that it would be left with unsold units of its already mature 300 Series of small car. It was keen to introduce an updated version to cash in on the boom, but the manufacturer was reluctant simply to scrap all the old stock to make way for the new models that were already in the pipeline. Franchisees were not taking the old stock, as they had customers lined up for the new versions, which were easier to sell.

A 'sales out' incentive was created that offered cash rewards to sales managers for achieving specific unit sales. In practice these rewards would be shared between the individual sales teams depending on their local performance. Cash had always been the preferred reward choice. But sales management had been lobbied to provide something more prestigious, with 'trophy' value, as the old stock was proving difficult to shift.

The idea of chartering the Venice Simplon Orient Express was put forward by the promotional agency, with the title 'The Sales Express'. The top 50 dealership owners would be split into 10 same-size leagues, and the top five performers against target would qualify with their significant others for a four-day trip, London to Venice, staying at the Hotel Danieli in Venice, with flights back for the return journey. In addition those who completed half of their target by the middle of the qualifying period would receive Orient Express branded luggage. This would be the first time that dealership owners would be specifically offered any kind of non-cash reward.

The results were astonishing. Market share for the incentive period of three months rose from 2.66 per cent to 4.5 per cent, which represented an increase in 300 Series unit sales of some 23 per cent. The rise in sales out was so spectacular that it merited a headline in the *Financial Times*: 'Incentives Help Volvo Reach Record Sales' (Kenneth Gooding, 6 June 1986).

Other automotive incentive hybrids

Automotive incentives are well documented and easy to track, as car sales are discrete units and publicly reported, both through manufacturer figures and through trade audits. In the Introduction, we cited

Mazda Motor of America as the classic automotive case study to show that non-cash rewards work better, dollar for dollar, than cash rewards. The overall performance improvement of over 15 per cent increase in unit sales is yet more testimony to the enduring value and return on investment (ROI) of straightforward sales incentives.

But incentives are not only popular ways to 'move the metal'. Many automotive franchisees can make more money from peripheral sales such as finance, spare parts and accessories than they can from selling the main units.

BMW Series 10 incentive

BMW Financial Services, Spain, launched a product incentive programme in January 2006 aimed at dealer distributors. The aim was to sell more finance-related products to BMW car buyers than previously. Car buyers are almost always offered a choice of finance to assist with car purchase, and even though they may be buying a BMW from a BMW dealership there is no obligation on the dealership to only offer BMW Finance – the brand has to compete with other, independent finance providers.

The sales programme was designed to cover all divisions of BMW Finance, including individual purchasers, new and previously owned cars and fleet buyers. Salespeople had to accumulate points during the campaign period, which could be exchanged against 360 everyday merchandise products online such as electronic items and watches. The top 20 points accumulators earned an exotic individual holiday for two to such places as Marrakech, South Africa and Cambodia. In terms of business achievement overall the incentive produced an additional 10 per cent of revenue target, with a 93 per cent engagement level and almost 1,500 registrations from participating outlets.

American Honda Motor Company and Fiat Auto, Europe

Even extended warranty rates can be improved through the careful use of an incentive programme. The 'Winners Circle' leveraged the Honda expertise in motocross bikes and rally circuit involvement, offering 35 specific merchandise items plus 'grand prizes' of holidays for the very top achievers. The programme lasted a full year, but thanks to some innovative interaction such as voice recognition redemption and random awards the programme produced an increase in warranty sales of 40 per cent.

In the 1990s Fiat Auto used localized aftersales incentives to promote sales of parts and accessories at specific times of the year – winter checks, summer holidays – to support the need to get purchasers to return to their dealerships for any add-ons, upgrades or repairs rather than buy direct or use an independent dealership. On one occasion points accumulated from sales facilitated the drawing up of rank order tables through which the top 5 per cent of aftersales managers, some 50 qualifiers, were invited as a group to Paris for the weekend as a reward for exceptional achievement.

The technique of a hosted travel group can be a very powerful way to motivate those participants with the greatest capacity to improve, with the added benefit of long-lasting memories of a unique event that stay with the leading distributor network for many months and sometimes years, if the post-event promotion is done well. The activity covered the entire year, and had different promotions for different parts of the aftersales network, with the idea that continuous but varied incentives kept the Fiat name alive in the minds of dealership employees and fostered an atmosphere of 'What next?' whenever Fiat aftersales products were mentioned, especially within dual or triple franchisees.

(I am grateful to the Incentive Performance Center, United States for the BMW Spain and American Honda examples, of which there are many more; see www.incentivecentral.org.)

IT and all things electrical

Automotive incentives have been around for more than 70 years in various guises and probably are the most well known of any type of incentive programme, whether they originate in the United States, Europe or the Pacific Rim. The main reason they are enduringly popular is the fact that the product margins for automotive products (including unit sales, aftersales and finance from the same customer, taken as a whole) are usually good enough to be able to allocate relatively large rewards per sale.

There is a similar commercial scenario within the IT, telecoms and electronics sectors, although incentives tend to be skewed towards distributor employees rather than retailers themselves. Programmes range from one-day 'spifs', which involve instant incentives for that day's sales activity, to long-term loyalty schemes and recognition 'clubs' to promote better engagement with a particular manufacturer's products and services.

IBM Circle of Excellence

IBM's eServer division was tasked with introducing a new generation of server products through its key third-party resellers. The Circle of Excellence was an online group of high-performing resellers who earned enhanced levels of training and IBM sales support by virtue of their commitment to IBM products and their active engagement in any promotions being offered. Points were awarded for sales in various categories, which could then be exchanged for personal rewards or pooled for the team's use, such as celebration meals out of the office or attendance at industry training courses. During the year when the programme was revamped to be totally digital – no printed registration forms to complete, performance updates instantly available, with online links to training resources – the eServer division recorded a 42 per cent increase in sales. This wider base created a much improved platform for future sales and market penetration.

Lucent Technologies: 'It's All About ME'

ME is the acronym for the microelectronics division of Lucent in the United States. They wanted a programme to capture all the great ideas that people get as they are working on projects during the day, with a view to improving their internal processes. In the days before the internet, suggestions and ideas would be collected through cumbersome paper-driven systems and discussed at length at specially convened meetings of technical experts to assess what ideas could work and what the costs of implementation might be.

The principle of the scheme was to combine recognition by peers – workers voted for each other to acknowledge exceptional performance against published organizational values – and cost-saving or revenue-generating ideas. Points accumulated were then redeemed against rewards in an online catalogue, and included individual holidays and leisure options. More than 54 per cent of the entire workforce participated, with some 6,000 ideas being generated. Of these ideas, 2,100 were implemented in one way or another in such areas as scrap recycling, reducing the cost of overnight couriers, improving plant safety and making e-mail more efficient. During the first year of this recognition and reward programme $20 million was saved in cost reductions or revenue generation, at a set-up and reward cost of less than $3 million, so it was an excellent result from an ROI perspective.

Sony Imaging

In 2014 Sony Digital Imaging Division ran a three-month, non-cash incentive campaign for independent stockists of their cameras and other digital imaging products. The objectives were to increase sales as well as the numbers of active participants who visited Sony Photo Zone, a private portal created by Sony purely for independent salespeople who regularly sold Sony photo products. The main product being offered was an Alpha camera. The aim was to engage with 80 per cent or more of retail store workers. Participants had to view online training videos and sell Sony products, with each activity qualifying for an entry into a prize draw for weekly items such as Sony electronic products and gift cards, as well as an end-campaign 'hero' prize of an Alfa Romeo car, based on cumulative activity. The campaign was called 'Alpha = Alfa'.

The results were remarkable. A 47.6 per cent increase in sales was recorded compared with trading for the previous quarter. There was a 27 per cent increase in individual participation compared with previous campaigns, and an 87.3 per cent level of engagement within independent stores. There were 1,181 training modules downloaded and completed during the qualifying period by registered participants. The success of this campaign was researched and found to be largely due to the effect of the portal communication offering targeted online training modules in specific Sony products.

AEG: 'Off to the Orient'

Dealer 'loaders' or incentive schemes have been the mainstay of promotional activity within retail networks for many years. The electronics and electrical sectors are classic distribution environments, where the owner or manager and floor salespeople all need to be working together if a manufacturer is going to drive its products successfully through the sales chain.

AEG ran a four-month incentive travel campaign across its UK distribution network based on a league structure. The higher turnover distributors were put together in a same-size league, with lower contributors being placed in leagues of lower turnover. This structure helped the field staff to encourage more participants than normal, as they perceived more stockists had a chance to win through to the level of the big rewards. A specific number of places for an AEG-hosted incentive trip to Hong Kong were offered per league, with bigger distributors having a better pro rata chance to win their league than smaller distributors. This overcame the concern that the organization should be rewarding those business partners who did more to sell AEG products aggressively.

Those distributors who achieved target during the first half of the programme qualified for a long weekend in Amsterdam. Lower-level salespeople won merchandise awards through a prize draw mechanism using Chinese fortune sticks. Provided they had sold the required amounts of AEG product for that period the field representatives distributed fortune sticks for each incremental sale made – the more they sold, the more chances they had to win the interim rewards. In terms of performance the top distributors increased their sales by around 20 per cent, with a few exceeding 50 per cent. The leaguing system, supported by a fast-start mechanism, was instrumental in achieving this very creditable performance.

Gaggenau: kitchen appliances

Independent retailers and kitchen designers were enrolled in a programme that rewarded the sale of specialist refrigeration units over an eight-month period with the invitation to the Ice Hotel in Sweden. The 50 winning participants enjoyed a variety of Nordic-style activities, including dog-sledding, snowmobile excursions, ice fishing, Lapp cuisine and a barbecue based around a Sami tepee. Sales improved by 50 per cent over the same period for the year before.

Some characteristics of sales incentives

It is clear from just these examples that reward programmes work and can deliver anywhere between 10 per cent and 50 per cent or more of previous sales when no programme was running. But there are some caveats. Successful schemes are creatively themed, well promoted, structured to appeal to enthusiastic, positively motivated salespeople and full of feedback and reinforcement. We will be exploring how this can be achieved consistently in Chapter 4. It is rarely all about choosing 'the right travel destination'. It is much more to do with targeted communication with rewards that stimulate higher-than-average activity levels.

Sales programmes reflect human motivation theory in many ways. The reward structures mirror Maslow's hierarchy of needs with progressively aspirational levels of reward the higher up the pyramid you go. 'Beat your best' programmes tap into the deep-seated human desire to exercise skill and talent and to be seen by peers to excel at something. Communication is regular and periodic, so as to reinforce desired behaviour. Levels of incentive reward are often set to provoke above-average activity and to 'be worth' the effort. Peer group pressure can be a powerful driving force for higher achievement, so sharing performance levels mid-campaign makes sound motivational sense.

In general, sales programmes are used to leverage short-term gain, monthly or quarterly, from distributors who have a choice of whom to give their purchases to within a well-defined marketplace.

In-house sales reward schemes for employed salespeople tend to be longer term and geared towards annual performance, with a healthy ingredient of peer group recognition in the form of a sales honours club of some kind. But virtually all types of sales programme can be seen to be based on sound, research-based, psychological principles. They do not work every time, as there are too many variables within a commercial context. Overall, motivational theories form a good basis for structuring the offer of the reward.

Recognition programmes

There is an old saying in the motivation business that there should be no reward without recognition and no recognition without reward. If the sponsor is allocating non-cash rewards for above-average performance there should be an element of formal communication to recognize those who have excelled, as this provides a powerful inducement to repeat the effort next time around. Equally a recognition programme tends to get better share of mind and adoption if there is an element of reward in the programme. It does not have to be large or impressive. Even a token gesture removes the potential criticism by disaffected workers that it is easy and does not cost much to say 'Well done.' Rewards for performance underpin that the management team value any positive change in behaviour.

Recognition is a powerful psychological tool that can apply to most working groups. Although published examples of recognition schemes are fewer in general, almost all larger organizations in the developed world use hybrids of recognition schemes to enhance and improve processes at work that would otherwise remain unacknowledged. Recognition programmes tend to fall within three types: day-to-day, informal and formal.

Recognition programmes are generally much more bespoke and relevant to specific organizations and to their full-time workers than those devised for sales executives. Outputs are harder to measure than they can be in sales environments. It can be done, but only a minority of organizations actually do so. Teamwork and an overall improvement in engagement levels tend to be the underlying measures of success. According to the WorldatWork (2008) survey, 89 per cent of the organizations surveyed ran some kind of recognition programme but only 8 per cent actually monitored any form of ROI. However, there are some useful case studies of recognition schemes that could be used as a benchmark for any scheme you may be thinking about.

Scotiabank

A leading Canadian bank, Scotiabank, embarked on a customer service strategy in the mid-2000s and supported it by implementing a sales- and retention-based incentive programme aimed at managers only. Although changes in the basic ratios of customer service could be easily monitored with this format, it did not produce the results they were expecting. They were disappointed.

After some research they realized that if customer interaction with Scotiabank employees was the main reason why customers stayed with a bank in the longer term they should redesign the programme to recognize exceptional customer service from employees at the point of customer interaction. They began to measure customer interaction rather than the cold, hard managerial numbers. Scotia Applause rewarded relationship-building behaviours, including interaction with the online customer service portal, measuring examples of excellent customer service and redemption of rewards for ongoing milestones of achievement.

These actions were then related back to the overall measure of customer satisfaction. It was found that the higher the scores for active interaction in the programme, the higher the eventual customer satisfaction scores became. The metric for success was therefore employee participation in the scheme. They proved to themselves that individual recognition of employees for active involvement in the programme was the key to improving perceived levels of customer service.

Delta Airlines: consolidating programmes under one banner

In the past Delta had run a wide range of employee group recognition programmes that serviced various divisions of the organization. They included length of service and retirement awards, instant recognition prizes, community engagement programmes, business revenue schemes, and a high-level honours club for 'exceptional service'. They were related to local operational needs rather than aligned to the business strategy and values of Delta as a whole. This resulted in mixed results for their recognition and employee reward schemes, with some VPs questioning their value to the bottom line.

All the existing programmes were then consolidated under one brand, My Delta, with success measured on the achievement or demonstration of their four goals, which were cost savings, customer service, operational excellence and revenue growth. ROI was 564 per cent of the cost of implementing the programme and any rewards distributed. Just as in the Lucent example earlier in this chapter, many recognition programmes are relatively inexpensive to create and manage and often produce returns that far exceed the original expectations of the steering group and the budget-holders' caution of what can be realistically achieved.

MGM: tracking better worker productivity

MGM Grand, based in Las Vegas, is a hotel property organization with a constant need to expand, replace and grow. In 2001 the management introduced a recognition programme for all employees, as they realized that everyone would have to make extra efforts to ensure the expansion was bedded in well. They emphasized the core values of the business as it related to excellence in customer service. Pre-shift briefing meetings from shift managers were introduced so that staff could discuss any service issues that were relevant to the coming shift. Token rewards and recognition notifications were produced for compliance with core values. The success of the programme was measured by the number of recognition incidents.

Over the years employee satisfaction, measured by surveys, gradually improved, and by 2005 the average score was 90.3 per cent. When you consider that most excellent engagement programmes score in the mid-80s this was a very successful scheme. By 2006 employee turnover was only 11 per cent, which is remarkable within the hospitality industry. The resulting bottom line was a 30 per cent increase in revenue compared with before the programme was introduced. Although it is always debateable whether the financial improvement was a direct result of this specific programme, as there are always many other initiatives happening within any large organization, there is no doubt that when managements place emphasis on core values and service levels the numbers follow.

The MGM example is reminiscent of the Hawthorne experiments (Chapter 2) in that by focusing attention on a few main behaviours people tend to pay attention and make an extra effort to comply, even without any significant personal gain. Peer group pressure to do what is being asked can be a very powerful influence when groups are working together. The trick is to maintain the communication of those requirements so that most people 'get the message' for most of the time, especially in an industry where temporary staff and shift work are the norm rather than the exception.

LV: engaging with your people

When employees appear not to care whether customer service is good, bad or indifferent, it is time to do something internally. Unless you have a high-margin product that is scarce and is always in demand, poor alignment with the goals of the organization and lack of a genuine interest in its success will result in decreasing profits and possibly the collapse of the entire enterprise in time.

Liverpool Victoria (LV) is a traditional general insurance enterprise in the UK, founded in 1846. In 2006 it was losing ground to more aggressive competitors, and although underlying profits were good the General Insurance division, the mainstay of the business, lost £22 million. This part of the organization employed the most number of people, taking inbound calls from new and existing customers, and numbered some 4,000 people.

A new senior management team was appointed and quickly concluded that the loss of 10,000 customers a month was unacceptable and identified that poor customer service was to blame. There was a pervasive, conservative culture of 'jobs for life' and that personal performance did not really matter.

The previous management style had been for the decision makers to stay in their offices and remain apart from their teams. Customer service representatives worked in a hierarchy of fear, with no organization-wide procedures for dealing with common customer queries, no way to recognize above-average performance, and not even any assessing of individual customer service activity.

LV embarked on a six-year programme of engagement initiatives based on a complete re-engineering of its internal culture and customer service processes. At the heart of this change was a new recognition programme called 'My LV', which allowed participants to congratulate each other for assistance, performance and even birthdays and anniversaries. Every employee could nominate any other employee, according to various rules and criteria, so the onus was not on the managers to keep the programme alive. Average engagement levels rose from 64 per cent to 83 per cent over a four-year period, and the number of policies being processed increased from 106,000 in 2007 to 708,000 in 2011. Underlying profits rose by 327 per cent during the same period.

Do reward and recognition programmes work?

What emerges from these examples of planned recognition and reward programmes is that if well constructed they work very efficiently. Sales-based or contingency schemes will produce incremental sales of 10 per cent or more in a mature channel where incentive programmes are the norm to perhaps over 30 per cent in a high-growth or new sector where sales incentives are unusual. If you wanted to set out a reasonable expectation for a motivation programme in terms of sales increase you could support a sales increase of between say 12 per cent and 18 per cent as the target. This would be consistent with most of the published case histories and research into what actually happens in the real world.

As for recognition schemes, they are harder to justify absolutely, but it is clear from the above examples that there is a strong correlation between higher engagement levels and better bottom-line profits. A number of surveys in recent years all point to the fact that better-engaged staff mean happier shareholders.

'A study by the global services provider Towers Watson [formerly Towers Perrin] found that high engagement firms experienced an earnings per share (EPS) growth rate of 28 per cent compared with an 11.2 per cent decline for low engagement firms.' This was the verdict of Allan Schweyer, whose job it is to conduct research into the effectiveness of the use of communication and recognition techniques for the Human Capital Institute (Towers Watson, 2009).

The common traits of successful reward and recognition programmes in action come through time and again whenever you examine the mechanics of such projects:

1 *sound research* into what the participants feel about such programmes and what has worked well in the past;

2 an effort to *retrain participants* in what they are required to do, whether that is to appreciate the new organizational core values or to sell new units rather than old ones;

3 regular, timely and individual *feedback on performance*;

4 consideration of *appropriate levels of reward* depending on the context of the programme and participant expectations.

It will come as no surprise to discover that constructing professional recognition and reward programmes follows certain principles, both to take advantage of other people's mistakes and to minimize the risk of failure when the programmes are launched. These principles are enshrined in the performance improvement programme (PIP) model or alternatively the business improvement programme (BIP). In Chapter 4 we explore this model, which you can use to set the agenda for discussion and debate when the issue of an organizational recognition and reward programme is on the agenda.

The performance improvement programme model

04

So, we agree that humans are all motivated in similar ways and we have seen some examples from different business sectors of effective reward and recognition programmes that work and seem to deliver a measurable bottom line.

The next step is therefore to begin to build a consensus within your organization about what should be done and what areas of the organization need to be involved in the planning of an effective scheme. It would be useful to have a system that sets the agenda for action rather than simply think up some rules and send out an e-mail.

The performance improvement programme (PIP) model is a useful tool to cover all the bases for setting up a recognition or non-monetary reward programme. Each element will be discussed in detail in later chapters. The key issue is to establish a working plan that can deliver motivation and engagement improvements. We will also look at some structural ideas to make your scheme work harder, from leaguing and beat-your-best formats to fast starts and peer voting systems.

Changing the way organizations do things is not easy, but it can be made easier by checking that the logic for doing it is correct. One push-back from VPs for more reward and recognition budget is how it fits into the overall business plan – and surely we already do enough rewarding and acknowledging of good performance through pay cheques and performance bonuses? R&R fits neatly into the box called 'Total rewards', as you can see in the model created by HR specialist and author Michael Armstrong (Figure 4.1).

Every organization or business has a reward strategy, even non-profit associations. In mainstream enterprises the total rewards plan usually includes elements that are financial and elements that are non-financial. As you can see in Figure 4.1, the left-hand side deals with elements such as basic pay, market pricing, bonuses, employee benefits and superannuation. On the right-hand side are the non-financial items. The two elements heading up the right-hand list are non-financial rewards (non-monetary incentives) and recognition. They are outlined in bold in the figure. Clearly job design, development opportunities and even the work environment itself play their part in better performance, but the main non-financial performance management drivers remain better non-financial reward and recognition. Performance improvement is an important subset of the levers all organizations use to create and maintain success. An organization that does not recognize its workers or consider what can be offered as rewards that are not financial for process improvement is, at best, wasting its human resources.

The performance aim of all organizations, commercial or otherwise, is to improve any given situation. No one would deliberately set out to make things worse, let alone pay more for being less efficient. The plan, therefore, is to rally effort and resources around a few key performance objectives with the overall purpose of making things better than they were, ideally for an incremental benefit. There is a need for a model that takes you through the steps to consider before implementing any kind of business or performance improvement programme, which will act as a guide for the subject headings to be discussed and debated internally when it comes to reward and recognition.

The performance improvement model

The performance improvement model has four elements: research, skills, communication, and reward or incentive (Figure 4.2). All organizations have a history. Often when you construct a reward or recognition programme you are amending and hopefully enhancing something that already exists, so there may be many short cuts you can take to build an

FIGURE 4.1 How rewards and recognition fit into the business strategy

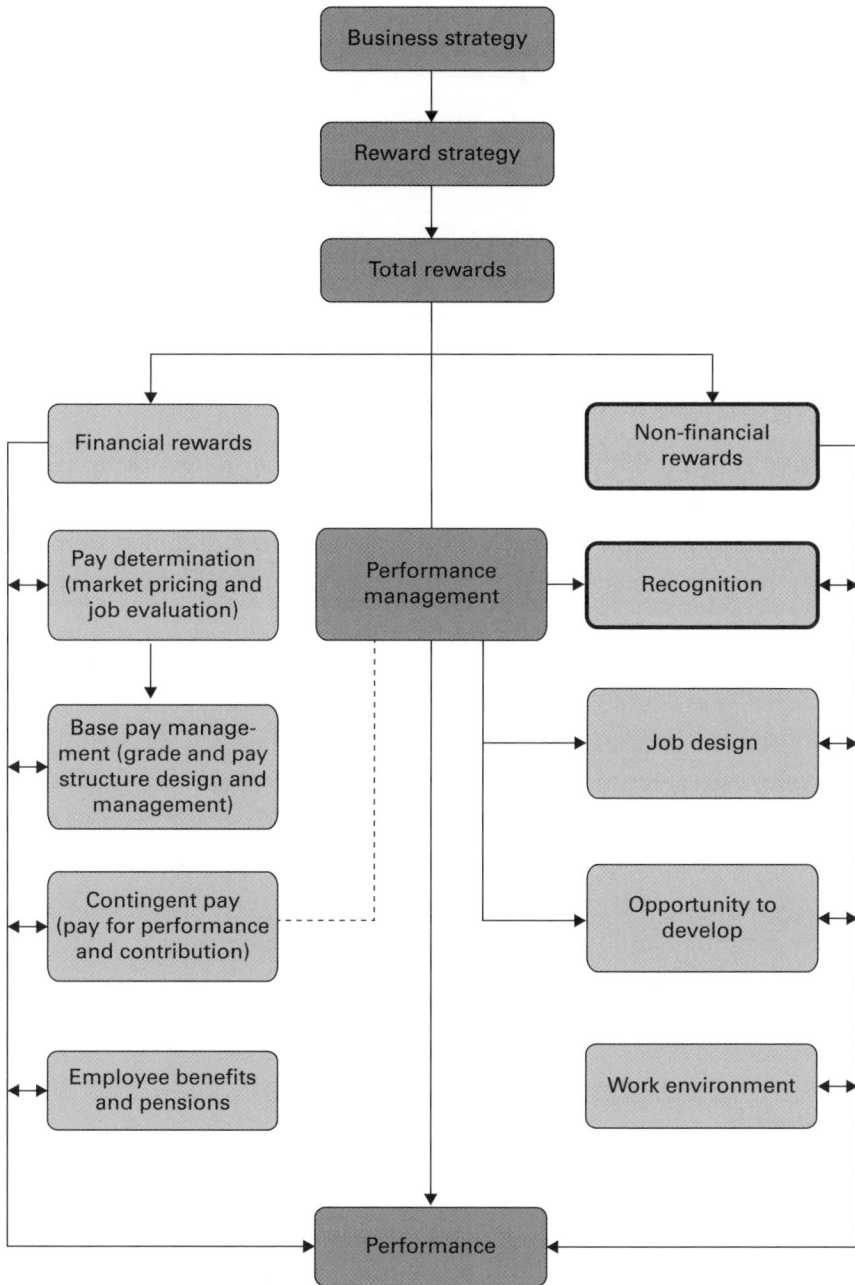

SOURCE *Armstrong's Handbook of Human Resource Management Practice*, 12th edition, Michael Armstrong

FIGURE 4.2 The performance improvement programme
(PIP) model

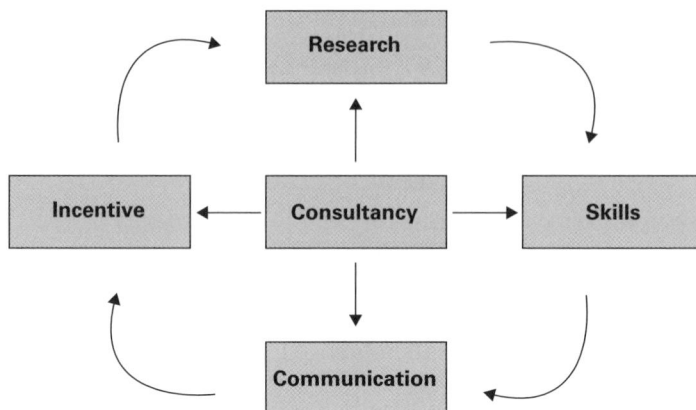

effective scheme. However, if the programme is not working in the way you expected, it is always worth going back to basics to see if a vital element was missed out in the design of the original system. Or it may be that it has simply become old-fashioned and you need to take a fresh look with new data.

If we accept the truism that many workforces renew themselves every five years or so, simply amending the existing scheme may be fatally flawed because many of the participants are now completely different. Mergers and acquisitions are classic cases in point where the old rules may simply no longer apply. When an organization acquires a new asset it not only takes on new people but changes its outlook on many aspects of policy. This in turn may well attract a new type of employee. Taking a new approach may reveal some insights that were not available when the original programme was set up, as markets and employee expectations change over time.

Research

Research can cover a multitude of techniques, but it does not necessarily mean you need to engage an outside consultancy at great expense or take part in complicated, industry-wide surveys. There are many ways to undertake the research element of performance improvement programmes, depending on the size of the organization.

There will be a lot of desk research that can be done to build up a picture of what has been offered in the past, what issues came up as a result and what changes you could make to make them more effective. Digital filing means that it is not difficult to go back say five years to establish the development of any current programmes to discover how they became what they are. Within any organization the personalities of the people managing such schemes often come to the fore. It may surprise you to find that some enhancements or indeed regressions came about by the ad hoc changes of the manager in charge of the scheme rather than strategic reviews sanctioned from the top of the organization.

As with all such initiatives a change in one part of the process may adversely affect another part of the same system. But, because no one is looking out for it, the change becomes institutionalized and ignored. The administrative mantra goes that, if it is working moderately well, you should leave it alone. Administrators do not rock boats without extreme provocation.

Your sector of industry and the performance industry in general will be publishing data on a regular basis in case history format about the success of programmes that highlight rewards or recognition systems. It is worth reviewing these to see if there are any obvious lessons to be learned about what makes for an effective scheme.

To get a more bespoke picture of how your organization views the current reward and recognition programmes you will need to conduct in-depth research known as a 'human audit'. The full details are described in Chapter 5.

If you have an internal research or HR department they may well have much of the data you need already on file about employees, their behaviour and your organizational structure. They may have been asked to compile employee profiles for all kinds of reasons, such as a prospective merger or acquisition or a public offering. Ask about what is currently held in the files about your work teams before spending additional budget on information your organization may already hold. Once you have reviewed the current situation and taken on board any specific criticisms you will then need to examine whether your current team has the right skills to improve on what happens now.

Skills

Encouraging improvement suggests that participants already have the skills to improve. There is no point in offering recognition and discretionary reward if people do not have the technical skills to do a better job. An assessment needs to be made of the technical skills of the potential participants and a plan devised to fill those gaps with relevant training and development. Such skills may include the knowledge of organizational values, how they might apply to that participant's working life and examples of using those values to improve individual or team performance.

If the new programme is emphasizing specific skills such as new product knowledge or an aspect of customer service it makes sense to offer additional support to raise levels of competence in these areas well before the programme starts; otherwise people will not be able to participate fully. In large organizations this could take several months, even if the organization has a good intranet. This is because the economic cycle may dictate that training or skills development activity needs to be carried out at certain times of the year to get full commitment.

If a major part of the new initiative is effective communication, which perhaps has never been a priority before, guidance for managers or supervisors in how to present information and follow it through may be necessary. This could involve a cascade launch where the main elements of the programme need to be explained in a series of workshops face to face. This all takes time, and examining the skills element of the scheme takes time and should be planned at the early stages of the entire project.

Communication

In terms of the relative importance of the four elements in the performance improvement programme model, communication is the most critical. It is a topic that dominates post-programme research and is the key driver in raising participation rates. An analysis of the current ways that participants are communicated with will identify gaps in the communication chain. Depending on the type of programme you intend to communicate you may need to think about new content for the intranet, a rewards website, an app for mobile phones or tablets, or offline media such as printed brochures and wall charts. Should you go down the route of closed-loop social media you will have to consider what messages to send and when to send them and indeed who will send them. There may be a claiming procedure, which will involve some element of initial registration of the participants and completion of basic data. There may also need to be a robust interface with external data if the 'performance' measures rely on outside reporting, industry research or verification of sales, for example.

Of all the elements that tend to be handled less well within performance improvement programmes, communication is cited most often as 'could be done better'. There is always a balance to be struck between providing too much information and providing too little. Cost can also be a factor, as no budgets are bottomless. The other critical element is creativity. It has to be said that most HR-inspired internal communications need to deal with mundane matters such as holiday pay, benefits and superannuation changes. This does not always lend itself easily to an arresting, creative treatment. The problem is that the mechanics of creating HR information, such as using the in-house studio or following a tried-and-tested format for briefings, often results in little consultation on how the item should look or the language used in the communication piece about the performance improvement programme. What started out as a ground-breaking, attitude-changing initiative can degenerate into 'just another e-mail' and so lose its impact and business rationale.

There is also the important issue of who is sponsoring the message. However well the words are crafted and illustrated, direct marketing research tells us that after the opening sentence most readers glance down (or up) on the page to see who sent the message. For improvement programmes to be effective the sponsor needs to be as high up in the organization as possible – the overall business leader would be good. This suggests that the message will therefore be perceived as more important than it otherwise would be, and participants as well as managers will take more notice of it.

The final element of the performance improvement model is probably the most talked about but in effect the least important – the reward.

Incentive/reward

There needs to be some benefit for participants to get involved in the programme. If there are to be rank-order tables of performance or simply recognition of a job well done, an appropriate reward needs to be promoted and explained. In Chapter 8 we explore what typical reward choices there may be. Reward is a complex area. Too little and participants do not engage with the programme and perceive that if the organization is unable to dedicate even a token amount for reward then the initiative cannot be very important. Too much and most people will consider the 'prizes' to be a waste of money and employees would prefer an across-the-board pay rise instead. It is a question of perceived value rather than the actual value of any rewards offered.

Rewards delivery needs to be thoroughly researched. For small groups, distribution of rewards by hand, face to face, can be very effective in terms of building peer group bonding. But large groups of 'winning' participants require an accurate tracking and distribution database so that any disputes can be resolved quickly and the budget can be controlled. It may also be that the frequency of rewards needs to be monitored by line managers who will need access to the data in order to do this. Statistics about reward claimants can be a useful tool for senior managers to gauge how well or badly the programme is being used.

Rewards involving travel or hospitality require careful set-up and management, so as not to disappoint or even worse prove impractical to provide. There is a long tail of logistics that goes with organizing events, starting with inviting the right people and including identification of their travel needs, organizing activities at the chosen venue and billing any additional charges after the final wrap-up. A badly planned reward event is worse than having no reward at all, as the story of things that 'went wrong' lives long in the memory and works against the concept of recognizing above-average performance.

Not all the elements are equal

When using models to plan budgets and timetables it is worth recognizing that although the performance improvement model diagram (Figure 4.2) shows boxes of equal size the workload and timing may not be as straightforward as the model suggests. If the intention is to do bespoke research of a large employee base the lead time is probably in the region of three to four months. If similar programmes have been done before and there are a lot of internal data available to draw on you could be ready to plan the scheme within a month.

Skills development is often the part of the model that has already been completed or alternatively you may be happy with the general level of competence and so no further people development action is required. This will be the case with most sales incentives where the majority of participants and the sponsors are fully aware of what needs to be done but are expecting the incentive programme to provide the extra impetus to get sales moving more quickly.

Communication elements are relatively simple to analyse and propose, but new digital software programs can take many weeks to produce and then a month or so to test. If you work for an international organization or one with many subsidiaries, getting agreement to the IT plan may take many months. If your communication plan involves an app or a new website rather than simply adding a few pages to an existing media channel the delivery could take even longer. Offline is, of course, a different matter, but most communications packages in the post-internet age are not based purely on print.

Non-monetary incentives or rewards are probably the easiest element to organize, as they are readily available from most suppliers. The exception is events. If part of your reward plan is to get people together to recognize them and celebrate achievement you need a physical venue or destination. Depending on the time of year some venues get very busy, so booking venues say four to six months in advance is not unusual for larger numbers of participants. This could be even longer for overseas venues that regularly deal with corporate groups, as they have a global rather than just a local market to service.

In addition there needs to be an operational gap between the end of the qualifying period and the date of the event. Once the names of the qualifying participants have been drafted there is often a validation process that sponsors need to go through to verify the achievements and check that the individuals are still employed by the organization, as personnel records sometimes lag behind reality, particularly in large concerns or where independent contractors are involved.

Typically there should be a gap of at least two months – longer if the qualifiers are travelling overseas – between the end of the qualifying period and the recognition event to be sure that all the validation of qualification can be done and the logistics can be planned. For example, booking international air tickets requires the sponsor to provide the actual names of people in the group before the booking can be accepted. Payment for air tickets may well have to take place in the same month they are booked to secure the seats, regardless of the travel dates. The booking dates need to coincide with the dates you are holding for the venue. So this process of tickets matching venue availability requires some flexibility and possibly some change, which is unlikely to be completed quickly or easily.

When looking at the performance improvement model as a series of tasks to be accomplished, the communications element is likely to be the item that occupies most of the time in work hours. You will need to set up and enlist assistance from your internal or external resources to ensure that everything can be achieved within the planned schedules.

Delivering the performance improvement model

Planning and implementing the PIP is not a project that can be delivered on your own with no interaction from others. There will be a number of internal stakeholders and sponsors who need to agree not only the plan but the words being used and the communication media being proposed. It may be that the programme needs to be tied into another organizational activity such as an annual meeting or the completion of a merger, so the optimal plan from your viewpoint may not be possible in the light of these other pressures. Flexibility and the calmness to be able to accommodate all these other internal pressures will be important as the project progresses.

In terms of external partners, there could be many if you do not have a full range of internal marketing services to draw on:

- research agency;
- HR consultancy to tease out the values and advise on skills development, if required;
- training supplier to roll out the main messages to off-site employees and other business partners;
- web and/or app developer, if part of the communications plan;
- graphic designer;
- copywriter;
- rewards platform supplier;
- gift cards or other reward commodities supplier;
- conference or event organizer;
- group travel organizer;
- budgeting support from the finance team;
- performance improvement or incentives consultancy.

In well-developed countries there may well be suppliers who provide most or all of these services for a fee. In other markets you may have to bring two or three suppliers together to achieve the overall improvement programme. There is always a trade-off between doing it yourself for no direct cost and asking a consultant to manage it for you. The cost savings of doing it yourself are probably outweighed by the extra time it takes to organize all the elements and the learning curve of coming up against all the new things that you will have to learn to pull the project together. The job of getting internal consensus is a task in itself. On balance, it would be more efficient to use an experienced programme organizer to set up and run new schemes. Once you have an established programme you may then wish to bring some elements back in-house, such as reward purchase, if only to reduce the handling fees that may be applicable for large reward budgets.

Is performance improvement an HR or a marketing task?

In large organizations the most efficient way to get things done is to specialize. HR are experts in people issues, their recruitment and remuneration. Marketing are good at branding and mass communication. The trouble with PIPs is that they start with people issues and end in communications projects.

When handled by HR, sorting out values and upskilling employees is professionally achieved in the vast majority of cases. But communication and managing discretionary rewards that are non-cash can often be a challenge simply because HR do not have enough experience with the mass communication skills required. Similarly marketing departments struggle with the learning elements of performance improvement programmes but do a good job in identifying what messages need to go to whom and through what media. In large organizations there may be an internal communications function that would be ideally positioned to create and run PIPs, and often they employ ex-PIP planning executives who bring leading-edge skills to an individual organization.

In most cases a judgement call needs to be made as to who may have the best skills to deliver the programme. In practice it is often a hybrid team of HR and marketing who come together as a project task team that is the most successful.

What type of programmes could the PIP model be used for?

PIPs do not always have to be a change management tool of strategic importance for the entire organization. The same model can apply to a localized process issue that simply needs fixing quickly.

When home loans group Bradford & Bingley were having difficulties in getting their customers' applications for home loans processed efficiently through their internal systems as a result of legislative changes, they decided to run a performance improvement programme that concentrated on gathering the correct information 'first time around'. Sales team members and managers were targeted to achieve a 95 per cent acceptance of new applications where previously they were achieving only around 70 per cent. To bed this improvement in, the entire sales team was taken off the road and spent two weeks being trained in the new administrative requirement. Gift cards were offered for achievement of the new standard, with managers being invited to a country manor weekend for the best performance within their region.

The programme ran for three months, and communication of performance against peers was every two weeks, showing rank-order

TABLE 4.1 Typical employee objectives

Reduce absenteeism.
Reduce costs.
Gather ideas for better efficiency.
Promote teamwork.
Promote interdepartmental cooperation.
Improve safety.
Improve timekeeping.
Increase productivity.
Improve staff retention.
Monitor project progress.
Improve budgetary control.
Recruit new team members.
Gather new sales leads.
Complete direct sales.

achievement. By the end of the three-month programme the average acceptance for the entire home loans division was 97 per cent. Because the skills had now been learned and everyone was aware of the need to complete applications accurately, performance of this particular process no longer required special treatment, and the reward programme was quietly dropped.

Performance improvement programmes are often used to support short- or medium-term objectives within organizations where straightforward coaching or mentoring has failed to produce the required results (see Table 4.1). For employees who rely on robust processes to get their part of the organizational task done, having separate programmes is a useful way to cross-check that what they are spending their time on is something the organization values.

If every organization's employees worked to their maximum at all times there would be no need for such programmes, but the reality is that many do not, perhaps because their supervisor has briefed them to do things in a certain way. Or it could be that a major organizational cost issue such as retention of employees is not recognized as being 'important' within a team's context of work for that section. Performance improvement programmes help both managers and team members sort the desirable from the essential, often with dramatic results for the bottom line and the efficiency of the organization.

Getting started: the human audit

Now that we understand the performance improvement model overall and how it can help in pushing through major changes in any organization we need to get started. The first element is researching your participants. This process is often known as the 'human audit'. It is a review of the profile, skills and capability of your workforce, gathered in such a way that you can then start to make changes to their performance.

Know your people
The human audit

05

If you have worked for an organization for many years you may think you know your people. The truth is you probably know a small peer group very well but almost nothing about the people who work in other parts of the enterprise, in different sites and especially in different countries. Age and educational background often dictate whom we communicate with on a regular basis within organizations, and so our personal view of what would motivate specific groups of people is often skewed and rarely objective. This is even more striking within the C-suite, where status and personality can often override true enquiry into the nature of average worker behaviour. The rush to find a solution to the problem needs to be resisted.

Performance improvement programmes (PIPs) cannot be constructed without doing some research into the people who will make it happen. In the case of human behaviour this suggests you need to research the actual participants so that you can deliver a scheme that will have the best chance of being effective when it is introduced. This is known as a 'human audit'. There will be some desk research to conduct, but in the main what you really need to know is what different types of worker think about past and current efforts by the organization to reward and recognize above-average performance. The key elements of any new programme will be obvious once this task is complete, so you can be confident that when it is introduced it will be supported by most participants.

Context is everything

Everything has a context. You will need to examine where your organization fits in the marketplace. Are you a leader or a follower? Are you independent or part of a wider group? Does government legislation impact on your activities? Are you established or a new entrant? Are you growing or declining? All these assessments have an impact on how your people will comply with any new programme. If they feel it is irrelevant or not the right time in the market cycle then they will not participate fully so you will have wasted resource in developing the new idea.

You may find there is considerable internal resistance to delving into the personnel data and opinions of individuals in anticipation of stirring up perhaps old grievances that managers would rather leave alone. In some process or manufacturing areas you may find that managers will claim they are 'too busy' to be providing information or time for what may seem to them to be 'just another HR initiative'.

Management style in your organization may be focused on delivery rather than change. Some supervisors will actively resist any attempts to try to change the status quo. This is one reason of many why the positive endorsement of the business leader is not only desirable but essential if your programme is not going to fall flat before it is even launched. Cooperation from the very top is key to introducing a performance improvement programme. Getting strong commitment to the project, even at the initial research stage, sends a message that it is an important organizational issue that needs everyone's support if it is going to be effective.

Company and sector performance

Public and industry surveys will tell you what market share you have in your overall sector, where you rank, what your position was say a year ago or during the last business cycle, and a whole range of other comparative data. Is this useful for the human audit? It may be, if only to show that the management team is aware of market pressures and what their current reputation as an employer is. It is highly likely that your marketing function already has this information, which it will have needed in order to put together a brief to its various promotional agencies and media buyers.

Within the HR function, benchmarking surveys of recruitment activity, graduate training schemes and involvement in engagement issues all add to the body of data that will help you to define where you are, how the world at large perceives your organization and what your aims and ambitions should be for better performance. The HR function will also uncover whether your workers are likely to be feeling confident about their future or cautious. If there is a lot of competitor activity in terms of mergers and acquisitions or there is general shrinking of demand for your particular product or service the reward and recognition programme needs to take this into account. Exit interviews can be particularly useful snapshots of what your organization does right or wrong, as leavers have nothing to lose and are likely to give you some hard truths about what you can do to improve things.

Personnel inventory

Within the HR function there are many sources of employee information that the research services provider will need in order to be able to set up meaningful samples across the organization. This information may need to be reorganized to be of specific use. It is likely that the research services provider will want to segment groups within divisions by age, sex, length of service and function. The views of an employee who has been with you for 10 years are likely to be very different from those of employees with less than a year's service, as will the views of those in warehousing and those in say marketing. One of the most productive splits of data will enable the difference in attitudes to be shown between managers or supervisors and individual team members. It is quite common to get a fairly bland and slightly positive view of a people topic from managers followed by quite a poor rating from individuals. The two findings need to be moderated and reconciled into statements that are true. This can be done only with reference to the status of who is saying it.

As the samples will be anonymous the data need to be organized in such a way that participant names are excluded. One way to do this is to randomize employee roll numbers into different but same-category lists so that you retain the integrity of the sample. Because HR data are collected and used for purposes other than research it may take a few weeks to reorganize the data into a useful file for research. Do not expect simply to have the file sent over and for it to be ready for use.

Research principles for employee surveys

Most developed countries have a professional research community that can supply useful services for those wishing to undertake specific research into employee attitudes. If you are fortunate enough to have an internal research function they can perhaps deal with the contracting of a specialist external supplier, as they will be familiar with the protocols required to hire a consultant and will be able to monitor the consultant's input and manage the billing process more easily. In general it is not recommended that you conduct the research yourself using your own employees. The principle of research is anonymity, without which individuals will not tell you what they really think.

Another deterrent from doing it yourself is the problem of objectivity. The added value of an independent research provider lies mostly in the fact that they are not 'insiders' and so have no preconceived opinions about specific parts of the organization or the attitudes of particular teams. This makes a big difference when it comes to formulating the questions. Questions can be genuinely objective, and the interpretation of the answers can be equally bias-free. In addition there is likely to be less 'leading of the witness' during the qualitative interviews. It is very hard for employees to tell a member of their own organization how things might be improved for fear of sounding critical, but they will be happy to sound off to an independent researcher, given the option.

The research process for the human audit normally breaks down into seven stages:

1 *Clearly identify the task.*

It may seem obvious, but the specific objectives of the research have to be agreed beforehand, as otherwise the results will be flawed. You may need to find a measure of attitudes to organization-inspired recognition programmes, why the distribution team has low levels of participation, whether the reward amounts are too low, whether participants understood the rules of the offer, how easy the rewards were to redeem, how long the programme should last and even whether people consider it to be a good idea in the first place.

As in all research initiatives there is a danger of 'mission creep' in which other departments might request that the participants are asked other, unrelated questions while the survey is under way. If you use the PIP model as the basis for your list of questions the research is more likely to produce the answers you require. Any questions that do not fall within the four elements of the model (Chapter 4) are unlikely to be central to the research and so should be resisted.

2 *Design the research.*

The procedures and processes involved in carrying out the research need to be set out in a design plan. This will include planning the thread of the questions, covering all the key issues, creating a timetable for all the parties, allowing time for consultation of the initial results and working in partnership with the sponsor to draft reasonable conclusions and some suggestions as to the detail of the programme you are planning to deliver.

It is quite likely that once the first qualitative part of the research is completed it will reveal some aspects of research that need to be more fully explored. There may be residual issues from past schemes that have not been resolved by the organization, or there may be some technical issue that needs to be resolved, such as the involvement of part-timers or subcontractors.

One important issue is the timing of the research. It may not be practical to undertake research at the busiest time of the year or just prior to a merger, for example. In general a complex human audit could take at least two months to complete, with another month for analysis and internal decision making. This suggests that detailed research is possible only if the delivery timetable allows you to do it. Promising an annual programme that kicks off in January with research completed in December is not going to be practical. So in terms of the research design you need to clarify which element is more crucial – fully detailed research or the January launch date.

3 *Decide on the methodology.*

With the rise of e-mail surveys and the culture of constant feedback on consumer experiences that the internet now makes available there is an issue with survey fatigue. It is estimated that fewer than 10 per cent of all e-mailings to prospects in organizations are ever opened by their intended targets, so simply e-mailing participants as the single way to get a response is not going to produce the results you need.

The method that is most likely to be effective for a human audit is to carry out qualitative research to discover the key issues and then follow up to a wider audience to measure the strength of feeling about those key issues. These discussions are fairly low-key and moderated by an independent researcher who leads the group through the necessary questions and often follows up new issues if they were not anticipated in the original brief. A key skill for the moderator is not to waste too much time going over one contentious point. In addition there may be 'hidden' issues that come to light only when the finer details are being discussed. The researcher may then want to 'snowball' this issue and ask for other people to talk to about it if they are not present within the group.

Within this methodology process there are decisions to be made about recruiting the initial focus group participants, taking accurate records of what they said, anonymity issues, writing up the report, analysing and cross-checking what was said between different groups, and the format of feeding back the initial findings.

When the quantitative research phase is to be done you need to decide how best to capture large amounts of information, especially if there are some open questions ('What did you think of…?'). You may need to build in reminders and a token thank-you for responding, such as an entry into a prize draw, to boost response levels.

4 *Select a meaningful sample.*

To be able to say that what the research discovers is true of most people you need to gather data from a big enough sample. It is impractical to aim to have all the participants respond, as this would be both time-consuming and costly. There also comes a point for most audiences or populations when asking more people does not add to the overall view or attitudes of the entire population. There are tables you can consult that show how many people you need to sample to determine that the sample answers will be true of a wider audience of a certain size (sometimes known as 'purposive sampling'). For small organizations there may be no point in sampling views beyond the focus group stage as the views of a focus group of, say, 10 people will be very close to the views of the entire workforce of, say, 50 people.

You will need to ask the right type of people the right type of questions. This is known as quota sampling. Typically for a human audit you will need to talk to VPs, managers or team supervisors, and ordinary employees. Depending on the structure of the organization this may have to be replicated at other work sites. The point of doing quota sampling is to compare and contrast the responses from the managers with the responses of those being managed. It is a common finding in human audits that managers tend to be more conservative with their answers and generally support what happened in the past or the current status quo. Workers tend to use research as an excuse to vent their frustrations about things they do not like about the organization. But care needs to be taken to moderate these responses. Letting off steam is a part of occasional research and rarely implies there is a major crisis of confidence.

5 *Collect the data.*

One reason to use an external research agency is the ease with which they can collect and cross-analyse the human audit data. There are proprietary software programs that collect, sort and display information in ways that illuminate what was said or reported. This may be through charts, diagrams, graphs, bar charts and other visual devices. To create these representations from scratch using spreadsheets and standard software is very time-consuming and prone to error.

Data also need to be sorted into various categories to be meaningful. What the managers say about past recognition programmes may directly contradict what the actual participants thought. This may be crucially important in the design of the programme and needs to be highlighted as a difference in perception rather than rolled up into an overall number. If sample numbers are low in various categories the editor of the research may need to make a judgement call about the validity of the data from some subgroups.

6 *Analyse the data.*

To remove bias from the interpretation of the data it is better to allow the external research specialist to draft the initial report. Even though there may be mistakes of fact (you may have 10 external sites not 12, for example), they will produce an unbiased report into what participants really think. If you draft it yourself, it will be hard to stop yourself moderating the data to suit what you have already decided you would rather do in terms of the programme design. Once the information is collated and the report drafted you need to consider the best way to present the findings to appropriate colleagues.

It is likely that most of the findings will be sensible amendments to any existing scheme and a generally positive score for the initiative of undertaking some type of recognition and reward programme. However, the research may also throw up some negatives, which will need to be dealt with in a sensitive way. For example, under the cloak of anonymity, workers may report that their current leadership team is not rated very highly when it comes to seeking out recognition opportunities, although this would never have been mentioned in any briefings or reviews in the workplace. Such findings need to be taken at face value as a call to action rather than a criticism that needs to be edited out of the final report.

7 *Present the data.*

It is likely that the first presentation of the data will be within your HR or marketing team. This is an opportunity to sift through the findings and sort the information into accessible sections and audiences. It is not a good idea simply to run off bulky copies of the research and send it to the C-suite with an e-mail. This is guaranteed to ensure it will never get read. It needs to be presented with an aim in mind: to run the best reward and recognition programme your organization has ever had, for example.

At the strategic level the findings should be matched up to the organization's overall strategy to see where it supports what the business leaders are trying to achieve and where it falls short. An executive summary will be helpful. Some editing may be required to highlight the relevant information and indeed the appropriate verbatim comments to support the general findings. In terms of presentation some people respond better to actual comments rather than lots of bar charts and diagrams. So, if there are glaring mismatches between what the organization is trying to achieve and what the workers think is actually happening, using a suitable and hopefully compelling citation is a good way to get the main points across.

At manager level, statistics and graphical presentations may have more of a place, as managers will be interested in trends and splits to drill down into the detail. They will be accustomed to seeing data presented in this way. In general, verbatim comments are not as credible to managers, who may hear anecdotal comments every day and tend to discount many as being related to the specific problems of the day rather than a strategic comment that should be acted upon across the entire organization.

Individual workers will be keenly interested in their own area but not so much in the wider plan or the overall business goals. In this scenario reporting back on the research needs to take the form of bullet points and open discussion of no more than four or five general points. If these points reflect the solutions being proposed, even better. For example, if you know that one of the main improvements to your current programme will be to introduce an online recognition scheme for all employees then the research that suggested this would be a good idea could be highlighted and discussed. Or perhaps your basket of rewards for the existing scheme is too restrictive, but it is part of your plan to offer more choice. You could then highlight this aspect and invite further discussion.

One note of caution is to avoid any issues that you know the revised scheme will not include for whatever technical reason. You do not want to stir up a groundswell of support for a particular change if you know even now that you cannot provide it. The purpose of the human audit is to gather support for positive changes so that when they are made workers will remember the earlier discussions and see that their views have been taken into account. However, it may not be possible to include everything people ask for in one go, as every organization has resource issues and cannot always deliver the perfect solution.

Researching sales and distribution attitudes

Reward programmes for sales and distribution staff probably account for most R&R schemes in most markets. As sales reward programmes tend to be costly the downside of getting things wrong can be significant. Most human audits are probably conducted with a sales incentive in mind.

Researching salespeople requires specific sensitivity in terms of the responses. Whereas most employees tend to respond positively and in a straightforward way, salespeople tend to want to read between the lines and skew their answers to get the best possible scheme for them personally. Anyone analysing the responses needs to bear in mind this 'What's in it for me?' attitude when it comes to sales returns from research.

This tendency to slant the results towards their own interests comes up specifically in sections to do with what level of points or credits should be allocated to particular product areas, the number of qualifiers per category, the level of verification required for certain types of sale, the duration of the campaign period and the rules about receiving credits if you change jobs or leave the organization's employment mid-campaign. In general these issues can be easily dealt with as part of the campaign rules drafting, but when considering the results of the research from sales areas the findings need to be looked at with the wisdom of experience in sales management rather than taking any views at face value. I deal with the drafting of rules in much more detail in Chapter 7.

One easy win in terms of sales incentives is to poll people's preferences for reward choices. As most gift card options are now digital it is less important to worry about what specific retailers to partner with, as there are a number of online products that offer a wide range of redemption options for no more cost than providing tailor-made choices. But one aspect of reward that often divides programme planners is incentive travel. There is often much subjective debate about what destination to choose to make the biggest impact on performance.

There is always a trade-off between cost and value. Rio, Hawaii and Monte Carlo will always come top of most planners' lists of possible incentive destinations, but cost and logistics may mean that choosing such destinations is not always practical. One way to reduce the subjectivity is to ask the participants, as part of the human audit, where they would prefer to go. You can list the potential destinations that are on budget and logistically practical and ask potential winners to vote for their favourite. The one with the most votes becomes the chosen destination. This helps greatly when the programme is eventually launched, as the majority of the participants will have already named the chosen destination as their preference, so you get instant buy-in for a major part of the sales incentive offer from the very beginning.

Human audit in practice: Hotpoint/Creda white goods

The Hotpoint/Creda example of a human audit is a useful learning tool in how to conduct a typical personnel research project and what results to expect. I have reproduced some of the actual findings so you can see how to interpret what was discovered and how this translated into the proposal for the incentive programme.

After some years using relatively low-level tactical incentives to encourage service engineers to refer introductions for boilers and other domestic central heating appliances, Hotpoint/Creda (now the Indesit Company) decided to investigate the support for a revitalized programme that might include support staff and other people in the service delivery chain. At the outset the organization had identified the need to improve average productivity in terms of number of visits achieved during the day and to reward those who 'did that extra bit', as one of the managers described it. In particular the company was generating more customer requests for servicing calls than it could handle in a normal working day, but there was no budget for simply adding more service engineers. It would need volunteers to put themselves forward to handle these extra calls – but it would need an incentive to encourage those people to come forward. The management team were a little sceptical that incentives would work for their enterprise. They had tried them a few years before and the incentives had not worked – or so they reported.

It was agreed that the human audit would have a three-phase structure:

- Qualitative research was proposed using focus groups from the main categories to be canvassed. They consisted of small groups of about 10 people, conducted by an external interviewer with an agenda of specific points to explore. The sessions were recorded so that verbatim comments that were typical of the consensus could be captured and communicated in the final report.

- To measure the depth of feeling about the key issues, researchers then contacted a representative sample of workers by phone and e-mail where appropriate to verify that what the focus groups were saying was true and what level of support there was for some of the changes being suggested.

- The third element was to run a pilot or test sample that explained what the plan might be, subject to budgets, just to ensure that what was being proposed would be well received in practice.

Qualitative research

Seven discussion groups were held, four in the north and three in the south of the UK, to avoid any possibility of regional bias. Senior managers, area managers, supervisors, service engineers, customer care managers and telesales team leaders were interviewed as members of groups. In total 70 out of 850 relevant staff gave their views as participants in discussion groups.

The subjects for discussion included general attitudes towards non-cash incentives, measuring performance fairly, reward options, and internal barriers to introducing a new programme, if any. Some of the findings that directly affected the structure of any possible programme included the feeling that staff wanted cash rather than gift cards (even though it is known that cash is less effective for the organization), that the former payment levels were too small for them to bother with, and that some felt that the pressure to move on to the next job could compromise the quality of their existing work.

On a positive note they asked for the office-based administrators to be involved, as there was a strong element of teamwork to get distressed customers' issues sorted quickly – call administrators used their initiative to persuade engineers to make detours, for example, to be able to service emergency clients, and so on. They were also not great advocates of trying to sell warranties to new clients at the same time as fixing their heating systems, as they felt this distracted them from doing a professional job, however much the company wanted them to do it 'while they were there'.

In terms of barriers to introducing a new programme the groups all fed back that the rules needed to be much tighter than the previous time to avoid disputes and misunderstandings about what counted as a 'new appointment'. They asked for more regular updates on performance during the programme so they could see the effect of what they were doing before it was too late to modify their activities.

Quantitative research

The discussions showed that any new scheme would receive a cautious welcome but that a number of technical details would need to be changed from the last programme they had. In the quantitative research, 20-minute phone calls were used plus e-mail questionnaires to some 200 participants. Part of the process was to get a measure of what people thought of such incentive schemes in general, and they were asked to rate previous schemes on a scale of 'not very successful' to 'very successful'. The feedback on previous warranty promotions was less than flattering, with 82 per cent saying that they did not think it was a good way to sell warranties and that in general customers were not interested. From the participants' viewpoint there was simply not enough reward in the programme to make the offer of warranties worthwhile.

One important issue was the concept of getting an extra day's pay for committing to work for four extra days a month. This cash incentive was designed to mop up the backlog of customer service calls to raise general customer service levels and had been in force for a number of years. This was thought to be a good idea by 67 per cent of respondents and was generally supported as an initiative. In research terms this indicates that whatever the organization decided to do it should retain this specific incentive to encourage completing more service calls.

Pilot test

However logical the answers from research appear to be, you should still test the new programme, if you can, to ensure that all elements, especially the rules, are well understood. In this particular case there was a certain amount of reluctance to go down the 'incentive' route again, bearing in mind the disappointment with previous schemes. A local area test was run for two months to measure levels of understanding, how the communication pieces worked and what the effect on performance was. The revised communication piece in this programme that highlighted ongoing performance was perceived by most participants as 'very good', which suggests it would be successful if it was rolled out to the wider participants' base. Because performance updates were cited in the qualitative research as being problematical in previous schemes it was important to get this aspect right to get wide commitment to the new programme.

Interpreting the human audit

It is not always wise simply to follow what the research says. This sounds counter-intuitive but it is important to think strategically rather than simply construct a scheme from survey results. Participants often report that if only they were given more cash their performance would improve. As we will see in Chapter 8 there are many studies that show that non-cash almost always produces better performance in value terms than cash. Just because most people think something is true does not make it true. Often participants say that they do not care about recognition and that the reward for performance is everything. We know this is not true of most organizations, where higher performance is the result of better engagement techniques rather than simply adding more reward.

The main purpose of the human audit is to help you construct a recognition and reward programme that has a good chance of being successful. It will help you focus on the key elements of the performance improvement model and devise rules and a structure that are likely to be supported by the participants. In the final analysis you want willing participants who will go the extra mile to deliver higher performance in specific areas that are strategically important to the organization.

So, armed with your participant research, you need to start considering whether the other three elements of the performance improvement programme model are relevant to your scheme and, if so, how to incorporate them. The next aspect to consider is skills development, variously known as learning, development, training or acclimatization. Without an assessment of your participants' skills you cannot deliver authentic, long-lasting performance improvement.

Skills and learning for performance improvement

06

If we have conducted the human audit successfully we will have clearly identified who needs to be targeted with a performance improvement programme (PIP), what the incentive offer may be and what type of communication is likely to work better than any other. But before we embark on an all-encompassing scheme that offers attractive rewards for changing behaviour we need to stop and think. Do our participants actually have the skills to change their behaviour?

As we have already discovered in Chapter 2 not everybody is motivated in the same way. Individuals are always on a journey through their own motivation cycle, and individual circumstances are changing all the time. When you are insecure, you will look to 'find shelter', and so basic remuneration and routine are more important than peer group acceptance or lavish rewards at that particular time. Simply introducing 'more rewards' is not going to deliver improved performance for everyone.

Equally, each person has a different level of skill in a wide variety of tasks during the working day. To expect all participants in any given scheme to be competent to the same level across all the possible process tasks they may be required to undertake is a little naïve. Skills development, when it comes to reward and recognition, is about providing the appropriate coaching or skills to achieve the specific tasks set out in the performance improvement programme.

How do people learn specific skills?

Although professional HR and development managers will be fully aware of the range of external skills courses and internal coaching available to all staff, performance improvement programmes are often based on behaviours or processes that are specific to a particular task or objective. So, when thinking strategically about reward and recognition, we need to go back to basics. There will not be a public course you can send people on to fix things quickly. What you want to mend is probably unique to your enterprise. Many critical skills are learned on the job and taught to people by colleagues, not by attending a specific programme of learning or from some industry sector guru or development organization. Principles of process improvement are relatively easy to isolate, but they are very hard to apply in specific job roles where having willing colleagues is as important as the learned new skill.

According to Jeff Cobb in his *Mission to Learn* blog, 'Learning is the lifelong process of transforming information and experience into knowledge, skills, behaviors, and attitudes' (http://www.missiontolearn.com/2009/05/definition-of-learning/). This process is not necessarily classroom-based, nor does it always result in some kind of competency certificate. It describes an attitude to absorbing new knowledge that in the workplace is very useful so that the organization as a whole can develop and grow. The more workers who have the capacity to learn to change their behaviour as a percentage of the entire workforce, the more likely the organization will be more successful. Adaptation is a key characteristic of successful enterprises, as the market and the economy are always changing.

Learning styles vary with each individual, but theories of learning have been moving from outcomes to attitude change since the 1960s. When learning theories were being developed, most academics were interested in how learning caused change. Did people need to perform the task in order to reinforce the learning or were there environmental factors at play? By the mid-1990s Rogers had identified two contrasting approaches: acquisition learning and formalized learning (Rogers and Freiberg, 1994).

Acquisition learning represents all those activities where how to do something is learned informally by listening, watching or doing along with others. Many work tasks are 'taught' in this way, and even those who are learning are often not conscious that they are learning anything. Parenting and possibly running a home are good examples of acquiring knowledge without any formal 'training'. Some organizations unknowingly use this technique to 'train' people all the time and often see no need to use other learning techniques. The problem with using just this method is that some colleagues are less good than others at demonstrating best practice, and so learning the most efficient way to carry out a particular task can be a long and hard struggle.

Formalized learning is 'educative' rather than through experiences. This type of learning is what happens in traditional schools, where there is a facilitator who tends to go through the theory and principles of a specific task and then everyone undertakes practical tasks to put the learning into practice. There is a higher amount of conscious learning, as participants tend to be more engaged with the aims and objectives of the session and thus they tend to learn more quickly than through acquisitive learning episodes.

There are many situations where acquisitive learning merges with formalized learning in a continuous stream. It is not an easy task to separate one type from the other. Organizations that recognize that learning is a combination of these two approaches tend to have more skilled workforces because the acquisitive learning process is primed on a regular basis by the faster-working formalized learning so that most people, for most of the time, get the most possible benefit and as a result overall performance improves.

Bloom's three domains of learning

During the 20th century US educational psychologist Benjamin Bloom developed and promoted an approach to learning that combined knowledge, skills and attitudes (Bloom *et al*, 1956). This way of looking at learning is the bedrock of many organizational learning programmes today and helps educators to decide what the learning needs of specific individuals may be for each type of worker:

- *Cognitive domain – knowledge.* In the cognitive domain participants are taught the principles of a task, through theories and useful examples, encouraging discussion and debate about how the new knowledge may apply to specific work situations. Participants probably do not practise the skills in the sessions but are encouraged to try them out in the work situation and feed back to the group how it went and what further lessons were learned by trying to apply the new knowledge.

- *Psychomotor domain – physical skills.* As suggested by the term, this type of learning requires physical skills with new tools or products. Demonstration and practice are key parts of the learning process, which is unlikely to be achieved in one session. Putting physical components together and completing new administration forms are good examples of such skills.

- *Affective domain – attitude.* This type of learning covers the way people react emotionally to a change proposition. In commercial or organizational situations this learning opportunity is most commonly experienced within sales or representation teams, where a change of attitude may be required for a given situation such as a downturn or even an upturn. You may need to change the emphasis regarding the manner in which things are done rather than the purely technical specifications. Examples include the kick-off meeting at the beginning of a sales cycle, a motivational speaker, and a new product presentation to a group of distributors.

Bloom's *Taxonomy of Educational Objectives* (1956)

Going further Bloom went on to classify the process whereby individuals tend to learn with increasing efficiency the more they discuss and 'experience' the new change. Originally this analysis was designed as a teacher's guide to improving the competency of schoolchildren.

Pupils need to be taken on a learning journey in a sequence rather than just being given a single session about the entire issue and hoping for the best.

The first task is to encourage recall of basic information. The next stage is understanding concepts, having learned 'the facts'. The third stage is applying the new skill in a similar situation. The next stage is to discuss the outcomes and analyse how the relationships between the component parts have changed. Participants are then asked to examine the effect of the changes or new knowledge in their given situation with a view, finally, to generating new ideas or ways of looking at different situations in the light of what has been learned.

It is plain to see how this sequence of how we learn best at school could be applied to the development of an organizational change briefing, particularly involving group discussions and feedback options. The basic information could be briefed on the intranet or by e-mail. This would then be followed up by group briefing sessions supported by visuals and examples. There could then be simulated sessions on applying the new change to the current process, using fictitious case studies and worked-through examples by technical people. Finally the process change would be implemented with a mechanism for feedback from operating 'as normal' so that the new system could be finely tuned to be more efficient in the future.

Workplace learning

Workers being sent on courses was the standard approach to spending the training and development budget in large organizations, but since the internet the delivery of learning has become much more diverse. In the 1980s it was true that the majority of workplace learning was classroom-based, with printed workbooks as the supporting tools. From the mid-1990s online training took the place of many residential courses for basic skills. Blended learning then took over after 2000, with open-source learning management systems (LMS) combined with classroom settings to obtain the best of both worlds, but the main characteristic was still information and direction being pushed out to the audiences from a central, authoritative point.

In the last five years the development of social media has meant that online collaboration and debate are now possible in a live teaching environment. Whether this method is more effective than standard classroom teaching remains a question. If by effective we mean less expensive then there is no doubt that delivering content online is almost always less expensive than asking people to leave their workplace and travel to a central location for skills delivery.

Learning styles: David Kolb

In 1984 David Kolb brought together many years of research from his own work and the work of other social scientists to propose four basic types of learning style (see Kolb and Kolb, 2005). Why is this important? It helps greatly in the design of skills development teaching to realize that not everyone learns in the same way and that to get a message across the educators need to be aware of how to put messages across efficiently within a diverse workforce:

- *Accommodators* prefer hands-on experience rather than theoretical training characterized by lectures and teacher-led presentations. They prefer interaction and trying things out, so a collaborative approach in which new ideas can be trialled with feedback on the reactions will suit this type of learner. Learning might be online or classroom-based, provided the opportunity to share experiences is available.

- *Divergers* learn by thinking about how the principle might apply across a whole range of experiences. They are more likely to ask 'Why?' than 'What if?' (unlike the accommodators) but prefer non-confrontational experiences and constructive criticism. Putting them up front when you know they will fail at a particular task causes divergers anxiety, and in those circumstances they will tend to withdraw rather than cooperate.

- *Convergers* will try out new ideas in stages and make small iterations to make something perfect. They prefer facts to theories and tend to work alone until they are comfortable that they have understood the new task perfectly. They prefer computer-based learning, as the pace is normally under their control, and they will be less distracted by the interference from other people in the classroom situation.

● *Assimilators* prefer the lecture environment and like to think rather than act in haste. Structured and organized learning with experts in their field is the best way to get results for this group, as well as discussion sessions where they can hear other people's views on the thing being taught. It comes as no surprise that senior managers favour this method, as they will probably have attended a tertiary course at university or its equivalent and will be used to the format of listening to or reading authoritative sources and then coming to their own conclusions as to how to apply the learning in practice.

It is, of course, virtually impossible to get workers to identify themselves before a learning session as to which category they fall into. The point is to be aware that a style that it suits you to deliver, such as the standard classroom teaching style, may not be suitable for the subject or task being outlined or for many of the participants in the room. Simply acknowledging that people learn in different ways should encourage the educator to mix things up a little and deliver the content in a variety of ways to take note both of learning styles and of the three domains of learning.

Learning and practical performance improvement

But this is not a book about strategic learning. How does learning theory relate to strategic task improvement? By understanding the rudiments of learning theory we can make the skills element of the four-step process more effective.

So what would be typical skills requirements as part of developing an effective PIP? They tend to revolve around administration or worker tasks and sales tasks. Let's look at worker tasks first. We have already seen some typical employee objectives in Table 4.1, which lists the most common objectives or issues that a PIP may seek to fix or improve.

There are a number of tasks in many organizations that lend themselves to reward-related performance improvement. In the broader examples such as absenteeism you can imagine that, following learning theory, this is a cognitive task and an affective task. Participants need to be aware that there is a problem, how much it costs the organization and that there is a need to do something about it. There will be some specific skills to be taught to supervisors about interviewing workers when they have been absent and the escalation procedure for persistent absentees. There will also be a section of skills development for managers around the issue of attitudes to absenteeism and being late generally and the effect it has on the workload of colleagues and team members when people are unexpectedly absent.

Within this 'skills' activity there will also be an appreciation that people learn new skills in different ways, so the style of learning needs to reflect the likely audience. If people are mostly well educated and managing teams, a lecture-style presentation might be appropriate, perhaps emphasizing the cost to the organization. If they are shop-floor workers, it might be appropriate to go through examples of how persistent absenteeism causes problems for their colleagues and communicate simple rules to report absenteeism using wall posters or simple graphics of statistics.

Ideas or suggestion schemes have been the mainstay of most large organizations, which recognize that their own workers are best placed to provide service improvements because they are completely involved with the processes concerned rather than trying to manage them remotely from on high. Learning theory helps us to identify that this is probably a psychomotor skill in that there is a process to go through to make a suggestion, which can be reinforced through rewards. The learning process would be a workshop approach with lots of interaction as participants try out what they might consider to be new ideas and the moderators agree or disagree and coach them to follow the process of how to submit successful ideas and suggestions.

One interesting development has been the introduction in some major corporations of 'future lounges', where employees can go to think about innovation or simply be exposed to new ideas and perhaps have a few of their own, having had a dialogue with colleagues both online and offline. Rohit Talwar, CEO of Fast Future, has been instrumental in devising and tracking the success of future lounges, which are based on specific research into how employees prefer to contribute their ideas for improvement in organizations. Similar to a relaxing area, a future lounge has visual displays and records of all the new ideas that the organization is working on, with staff available with whom people can talk about their new ideas. The ideas do not have to be about new products or services. Suggesting ways to improve the way the organization works is also valid, and the ideas implementation team are there to get ideas assessed and implemented if they can be made to work.

Recruitment of new staff is an expensive business for many organizations, especially if the economy is growing and employees are looking to move rather than to stay. It is well known that often the best recruits come from personal recommendation, so asking current employees for details of their friends and relatives makes good commercial sense. In terms of learning, this skills task is cognitive in that there is a simple process to go through that requires little skill other than completing an online recommendation form.

Sales tasks can be equally challenging. Compliance with data requirements or reporting is something at which sales teams tend to baulk. Learning theory tells us that salespeople are likely to respond better to a system where they can practise before deciding on a solution. Confidence comes from learning at one's own pace rather than being pushed by peers to assimilate knowledge at the same speed as everyone else. There is also the pressure not to spend too much time out of the field doing traditional training, as salespeople could be losing income by being out of contact with their customers for extended periods.

Financial services learning example: attitude and cognitive

During the 1990s a large UK home loans organization was experiencing problems with the level of its compliance with new legislation. The legislation said it had to complete a 'financial fact-find' interview with new clients before making financial recommendations. This requirement needed to be a completed document rather than just notes of a discussion, with specific fields of data that the regulators needed to review in order to validate the individual sales licences of the various firm representatives.

The 300-strong sales team were used to selling in their own way and although they had heard and read a lot about the new legislation in the trade press they carried on as normal. Documents were only 50 per cent completed, and there was a general attitude that the office-based administration team could complete the forms through their records and contacting salespeople later in the process on an ad hoc basis. This was very time-consuming and caused much friction with the 'convergers' in the back office, who wanted things in their right place. Most salespeople were accommodators and 'divergers', who liked nothing better than pushing the system to see how far it would bend.

The first task was to run an attitude session, explaining how the lack of compliance was causing a significant backlog of work for the administration team and that redoing the documentation and clarifying data from clients were costing the organization a lot of money, which would mean high charges in temporary staff and the potential of further financial sanctions from the regulators. In extreme cases the regulators had powers to request that all sales representatives could have their sales licences revoked and be taken off the road until suitable training had been completed.

Once the issue was flagged up as a major organizational problem the salespeople were then taken through hands-on classroom sessions showing how to complete the documentation during a sale and measuring how well or badly each individual was doing. In this specific case an incentive was added of gift cards for maintaining a high level of compliance. The best performers of the new task in the salesforce, some 20 individuals, were then treated to a weekend in a Scottish castle for maintaining persistently excellent compliance in this specific task.

Owing to this combination of learning techniques and incentive, within three months overall compliance levels had reached average levels of 95 per cent. After a further three months management reported that very few documents were incomplete and that 'the lesson had been learned'.

Sales tasks can be equally challenging. Compliance with data requirements or reporting is something at which sales teams tend to baulk. Learning theory tells us that salespeople are likely to respond better to a system where they can practise before deciding on a solution.

Agricultural representatives: psychomotive and cognitive

A global manufacturer of farming equipment and accessories spent historically large budgets on sending local representatives to hotels for traditional classroom-style training on how to introduce finance and leasing products at the point of sale. For most representatives the subject of finance was not an attractive topic and had the aura of being difficult and remote from their normal role, which was largely one of 'show-and-tell'. Taking them off to a hotel with their peers and some financial experts for a few days provided plenty of scope for misunderstanding and loss of face with their colleagues.

As finance is a non-physical product, it was clear that some of the learning could be done online with the intervention of an online tutor if some concepts were too hard to grasp. Participants could follow the course at their own pace online and test their knowledge bit by bit until they felt confident enough to submit their input for formal review.

This type of course was particularly suitable for participants who were more practical than intellectual by nature and would be somewhat intimidated by a classroom situation with their peers observing their performance. The big advantage for the sponsor was the reduction in overnight hotel costs and the inevitable 'time off the road' within a very competitive market.

Evaluating the impact of learning

It is clear in the financial services learning example that the improvement in compliance was the measure by which the learning of the new skills was effective. But not every new task has such cut-and-dried outcomes. In the agricultural representatives example there would need to be some kind of post-learning research to find out if the new way of imparting knowledge was both more successful with the participants and more cost-effective for the organization than the former way of doing things.

Fortunately for us there is a strategic way to examine whether new training has worked. In 1959 Donald L Kirkpatrick published a series of articles about the four levels of evaluation as part of his doctorate (see Kirkpatrick and Kirkpatrick, 2009). A fifth level was added by Jack J Phillips (2011) to cover the requirement for commercial return on investment (ROI). The theory suggests that proper evaluation of learning can be achieved by applying some or all of these levels of assessment to any given skills intervention:

- *Level 1: satisfaction.* Participants should be satisfied that the development sessions are delivering what they expect to learn and with the way the knowledge or skill has been imparted.

- *Level 2: learning.* Did the learning transfer? Change in behaviour will not happen unless one or more of the key learning objectives have been achieved, such as new skills, new attitudes or new knowledge.

- *Level 3: impact.* Did the new learning have any significant impact on performance once participants had returned to their everyday jobs? This could be verified by observation, reporting back and interviewing candidates who used the new techniques or knowledge.

- *Level 4: results.* Taking all things into consideration it should be possible to see a change in business performance as a result of the new learning. This can be either at the individual contribution level or at the team level. For example, did processing of insurance applications improve as a result of the newly learned system? Did sales of the new product increase following the learning sessions about the new product and how to sell it?

- *Level 5: ROI.* It is one thing to make more sales. It is quite another to produce more sales at a profit. So the ultimate test of learning new skills for any enterprise is whether the skills intervention produced enough extra profits to cover the cost and produce incremental profits. Moving towards assessing these ROI results should help all organizations decide what the incremental gain will be in upskilling certain types of employee. 'Nice-to-have' becomes 'essential-to-do' if it can be shown that the organization gets a net benefit from doing it.

The performance improvement programme dividend

It sounds very daunting to have to become an expert in learning and development simply to run an incentive scheme or a recognition programme, but in most cases the non-monetary reward or recognition scheme requires a distinct and defined change in one or two behaviours to achieve its aim. The majority of PIPs are aimed at a specific change in process or attitude where the 'new skill' is something very specific such as knowledge about a new product or a change in administration procedures. A change management programme that attempts to change thousands of employees' general attitudes to their sector is a completely different type of project. It is important to keep things in perspective and not try to achieve too many objectives with what is largely a 'do this–get that' activity to fix a specific issue.

So, now that you have checked whether more learning is required and have either put the learning sessions in place or decided that more learning is not necessary, you need to communicate what it is you are going to do. When PIPs are researched post-campaign, the majority of the comments and sometimes complaints from participants are that, although the scheme was well organized and the rewards were competently distributed, the communication was inadequate. Often participants say they did not know what they were being asked to do differently. They may also say that the rules were not clear or that they did not realize they were supposed to be taking part in the programme.

In Chapter 7 we examine what good communication looks like and how to avoid the more common mistakes, not the least of which is the lack of budget allocated to internal communication in general.

Communicating reward and recognition

07

The third and probably the most important part of the performance improvement process is how to communicate with your audiences for the greatest impact. Unlike mass advertising or broad-brush consumer promotions, telling incentive participants how to gain a reward or congratulating an individual for doing well is a personal, one-to-one communication that should go directly to the heart of those being communicated with.

Reward and recognition programmes are about individuals and their personal efforts as human beings. For that reason the question of how to communicate reward and recognition is fraught with difficulties, problems and potential misunderstandings. At the heart of good communication is the appreciation of the target as an individual human being, so seeing communication from the point of view of the recipient is a key strategic skill.

Typically, rewards such as salary, cash bonuses and other benefits of employment tend to be communicated as a financial statement that simply lists what individuals are entitled to. Much time and effort are spent by HR teams getting these statements correct. Because they are personal and confidential there are many opportunities for error or confusion. People change jobs, are promoted, get demoted, leave the organization and then join it again. But in this strategic review of 'reward' our topic is discretionary incentives – in other words tactical non-cash payments – so in most cases the working out or payment of incentives is not straightforward and they are not an entitlement that the organization is obliged to pay. This makes the entire communication process very difficult, requiring a clear view of what the offer is, who should receive it and when it will be paid.

This process becomes even more problematic when we turn our attention to recognition programmes. It is usually quite clear how long an individual has worked for a specific employer, so calculating and communicating a loyalty, non-cash bonus should be simple. It rarely is. Just as with incentives, a change in status often means that basic assumptions about what 'the deal' is can be difficult to confirm. The larger the organization the more likely there will need to be a long list of rules to handle unpredictable circumstances. If the organization gets this wrong all the positive effect of having the recognition system in place can be undone by a brusque or hasty quoting of the rules only to find that there is no rule for this particular circumstance. Individuals, quite rightly, become very disenchanted if the organization reneges on its promises. For individuals or teams, the fact that the reward is discretionary and not contractual makes no difference to the feeling that somehow they are being denied something they felt they had worked hard to obtain. No reward or recognition scheme should leave participants feeling that they have been cheated in some way.

Communicating incentives

By far the majority of discretionary, non-cash reward activity is to do with incentives for additional sales or performance. Some surveys suggest this could be as high as 80 per cent of all non-cash reward expenditure, so it is worth spending some time thinking about what the audiences are for such schemes:

- At the highest level you will need the senior executives in the organization to agree that there is a good business case for allocating discretionary resources and money to a speculative activity that may or may not produce better results.

- There will no doubt be stakeholders in the organization, internal and external, who will support or reject the need for such activity. Typically you will need to appeal to the sales, marketing and HR communities to work with you to achieve a workable programme.

- There will be a number of internal managers and teams who will be asked to contribute to the activity over and above their 'normal' jobs. Incentive schemes that do not directly benefit internal employees often suffer from lack of commitment if people view the incentive as something extra being given to other individuals whom they perceive as being well paid anyway.

- If the non-cash incentive is being aimed at an external sales team such as a distributor's team or the field force of a business partner, the owners of that organization need to lobbied for their support and commitment. It may seem obvious that an external organization would never refuse something with no cost to them, but it is a competitive world and often distributors know they can make more sales by aligning themselves with a better-known product than yours and so the offer from a sponsor of cost-free incentives is not a foregone conclusion.

- Within the external partners there will be sales teams of various kinds, and they also need to understand and work with what you are suggesting in terms that they can easily understand and implement. If you make it too complicated to receive the rewards then they are likely to respond by not taking part.

- Finally, perhaps hidden in the background are the various teams who will be supplying the measurement systems for you to be able to run your programme. There will be a basic need to communicate performance during the campaign, not just at the end. If you need specific data feeds on activity or sales types, are the data analysts and providers happy to provide the additional data or should you simply construct your programme around what is already provided to the management team?

Getting top-level buy-in

One of the great advantages of the digital age is the speed and quality of market information. The scale and frequency of data are also its downfall. Senior executives are bombarded with reports and trend statistics, so the likelihood of getting agreement to spend more discretionary budget is low if the communication of that request is too complex or requires too much background reading. Large organizations may be accustomed to being lobbied by HR and sales teams to use resources for reward and recognition purposes because they all know from past experience that it works, but for those who are not used to deciding on such programmes the arguments can be hard to absorb.

The key part of all reward and recognition schemes is the expected return on investment (ROI). A full explanation is given in Chapter 11. In communication terms the returns over and above the expense need to be highlighted up front to the senior team. There are many examples in Chapter 3 that could be used to support the initiative. Your job as programme sponsor is to gather those examples that have the best resonance for those who are making the decision. IT organizations will welcome examples from the IT industry; automotive companies will like to see successful examples from the automotive industry. Even examples of competitor activity will be relevant, in terms of considering whether your organization is being 'left behind' or slow to react.

Another element could well be examples from your own organization of successful schemes of the past. Metrics to include are incremental sales, better productivity or higher market share as a result of running previous programmes. A purist may be able to say that the extra performance may well have been due to other factors such as having a ground-breaking product or a particularly benign economic environment. Lord Leverhulme was once reputed to have said 'I know half of my advertising isn't working. I just don't know which half.' It is the same for most marketing programmes. It is almost impossible to determine that one single marketing activity resulted in the overall success of an initiative, but the evidence shows that, if you do not do it all (advertising, in other words), corporate performance suffers.

Details of the programme itself can be just a few lines together with a nominal budget so that senior executives can see the general amount of spend. It is fair to say that executives who are not used to scrutinizing incentive budgets may well be surprised by the amounts of budget being asked for. Many budgets are based on large numbers of participants, so, although the fixed costs of communicating may be minimal, even a modest number of winners from a workforce of say 10,000 will be significant. Typical budgets for an annual scheme range from 1 per cent to 3 per cent or more of the overall remuneration budget for those involved, so in terms of risk the amounts are small.

The important point is that once the initiative is agreed the senior team should wholeheartedly support it at every public opportunity; otherwise the investment will be forced to work very hard to make a return for all concerned. Typically operations VPs tend to downplay the use of incentives, as many senior jobholders consider the work itself to be enough reward without needing to receive additional incentives. But the reality is that incentives work and produce a return in much the same way that product innovation produces a return. It would not make business sense to ignore a technique that produces higher profits for the organization and its shareholders.

Negotiating with stakeholders

Who are the stakeholders? In the context of communication the stakeholders are likely to be your own colleagues who want to run such a scheme and their external business partners. At this level the entire programme needs to be worked out in detail with fully thought-through designs, key copy lines, rules and a clear explanation of what the participants have to do to gain the various rewards. In the process of determining what the rewards will be and how many will win what, a budget will have emerged. (We discuss budget planning in Chapter 11.) You should also have worked out by this stage how to measure success and what the number of likely winners will be. Communication to this group is therefore likely to be more like a presentation with visuals as well as charts and tables.

If you need to involve external stakeholders such as business partners it is likely that they will have their own ideas about suitable rewards. Often they run many more promotions than you and may well have used some of your reward ideas before, so it is helpful to discuss rather than impose reward ideas with these stakeholders, and they will probably have more recent feedback on what works and what does not within their participants' database. They may also be able to identify some data collection gaps within their own organization that may need to be fixed before the programme commences. For whatever historical reasons, your product sales may not be recorded in a way that is compatible with your own management reports, so you will need to devise some methods to ensure that the data are robust to enable worthy winners to be produced.

End user communication

In marketing communities the end user is normally the consumer. In business-to-business contexts the target market is incentive programme participants. Unless they are your own sales team they are usually employed by someone other than the organization that is sponsoring the incentive scheme. Their culture is therefore somewhat different from yours. This means that the style and choice of words need to reflect what they expect to hear and see.

A 22-year-old selling electronic devices to consumers from a mall is likely to have very different expectations of the incentive from a 50-year-old manager of an automotive parts retailer. Whatever their profile they will be unlike employees who work for a manufacturer, so corporation-speak needs to be avoided at all times, particularly terms and phrases that tend to creep into large organization communications as a result of current initiatives and internal programmes.

Using fewer words rather than more is the watchword, and inventing a memorable title or logo device is what is required creatively.

Alliteration helps ('Go for Gold'), as does any combination of words that would naturally bring to mind the sponsor's identity. If for example Avis were running an incentive scheme for travel outlet representatives they might call it 'Trying harder – an incentive programme for exceptional performance', based on their corporate phrase 'We try harder'. Here are just a few examples of incentive programmes that have been used over recent years to illustrate the type of phrase that works well:

- Embark on Excellence;
- Question of Quality;
- Breaking the Barriers;
- Theory into Practice;
- Counting on Customers;
- Leading the Way;
- Future Perfect;
- Winner Takes All;
- Move On Up;
- Quest for the Best;
- Let's Go;
- Steps to Success;
- The Power to Deliver;
- People Matter Most;
- Going Places;
- Good, Better, Best;
- Ready, Jet Set, Go.

The better programme themes tend to come from the initial discussions about the main objective of the scheme and arise spontaneously when discussions about the objectives, the incentive rewards and the type of product being promoted are held. Often they are linked to a popular musical artist, song or television programme simply because they are of the moment and more likely to provoke interest and discussion.

Although there is no reason why you cannot use previous programme themes dreamed up by someone else or even used in a different industry sector it is always better to come up with your own unique phrase, as this tends to get talked about more than one borrowed from elsewhere. Whatever theme is adopted it needs to stand out from the normal project titles used within organizations so that it gets noticed. In the context of needing to work for a third party the phrase also needs to compete with other sponsors' campaigns, as business partners always have a choice of whom to do business with. If your theme is 'normal' then it is less likely to be noticed by the independent sales team than one that begs for your attention.

Communicating recognition

Incentives are normally aimed at independent salespeople and thus need to make a bold statement and be seen to stand apart from normal corporate communications. Recognition programmes for employees are much more subtle. Because the organization has a captive audience in that the participants are all employees the message can be less promotional and more personal to the specific organization.

It is likely that your recognition programme will be recognizing employees for demonstrating clear corporate values – this is the reason for having such a scheme in the first place. This emphasis on values lends itself to a different style of theme and general presentation. Here are some examples of recognition themes that link closely with the sponsoring company corporate values:

- Going the Extra Mile;
- The Best You Can Be;
- Service First;
- Ideas in Action;
- On Course for Quality;
- Building on Strength;
- Mission: Improvement;

- Make It Count;
- Committed to Quality;
- Values Added;
- Make the Difference;
- There's a Me in Team;
- Stand Up... and Be Counted.

Measuring performance for recognition can be difficult, as much depends on subjective views on performance and in some cases putting yourself forward for an award. Unlike salespeople, those who deserve to be recognized are rarely identified objectively by means such as sales or profit figures. For that reason, working out carefully and communicating clearly from the beginning of the programme what the criteria will be, how 'success' will be measured, who will decide who is to be nominated and what happens if you change your employee status are necessary to avoid embarrassing anomalies. In many cases the bigger rewards are reserved for allocation by an independent committee of senior managers to avoid potential mistakes or possibly self-serving supervisors. There is nothing more likely to dampen the enthusiasm of participants than an unworthy winner or systematic bias towards specific types of employee.

A further communications issue is to ensure that all parts of the organization get an equal say in the programme. For sales schemes you are normally dealing with an individual VP of sales or of the business partner organization. Within a large corporation there may be many more stakeholders with whom to have a dialogue in order to arrive at the best possible recognition programme solution. Many schemes are HQ-centric in that the structure of the programme and the way it is communicated are generally well adapted to those who work in the main office, but post-launch research often reveals that those who work in sub-offices or overseas or in partner organizations are less well informed about what the scheme is all about and as a consequence the scheme gets much less support and response than expected.

Town hall meetings, briefings and good presentation materials need to be produced to ensure that all parts of the organization get a fair opportunity to take part. This element of tailoring the message also applies to different functional parts of the organization. It is unlikely that a document to explain a values scheme to main office employees will be easily received by warehouse employees who work in large sheds in possibly remote locations. It is worth analysing whether there are specific parts of your audience who require a different type of briefing and campaign materials to take in the programme messages. You can imagine that the overall theme could stay the same but the words used and the presentation of the mechanics of the scheme could be very different for those who do not have constant, daily access to desktop computers.

What's in it for me?

Most promotional communication involves reducing a complex offer into as few words as possible without being misleading. This works well in consumer marketing situations, where you usually have a very short window to attract attention. The consumer has to perceive 'the deal' very quickly; otherwise they will buy another product. When it comes to reward and recognition programmes the participants have much more time to absorb the details, but the communication still needs to be clear and simple. Too little detail and you risk asking individuals to undertake tasks that have no bearing on the rewards, if any. Too much detail and employees will switch off and simply not participate. In essence reward and recognition programmes rely on well-crafted rules. Good rules explain in as few words as possible what benefit participants can derive from taking part and how to qualify for those benefits.

Strategic points about programme rules

It is not possible to cover all types of campaigns with a fixed set of dos and don'ts, but when communicating with your various audiences here are some pointers to bear in mind to avoid communication misunderstandings and possible complaints. Normally drafting the rules comes well before the creative communication and any

discussion about rewards. If you can tighten up this aspect of programme planning the promotional aspects and creative ideas will fall
into place when required:

- *Participants need to know when the programme starts and when
  it ends.* This may sound obvious, but it is surprising how many
  sales incentives, for example, are launched with no clear guidance
  on such vital measurement parameters. Specify the actual day the
  programme starts and the time for cut-off at the end for claiming
  performance or sales, having checked carefully that it is not a
  public holiday or a weekend. There may be certain claiming
  procedures for specific types of worker group, so spell these out –
  simply putting sales claims in the mail may not be enough.

- *Participants need to know what they have to do.* Make it
  clear what each participating group has to do to qualify for
  the various rewards. There may be more than one measure,
  or there may be a moderating aspect such as a minimum
  percentage of contracts confirmed before a participant can
  qualify for anything at all. It is standard for there to be a
  number of different types of participant following a different
  set of criteria to win the rewards, so each subset needs to know
  what it has to achieve specifically. It is not enough simply
  to say 'Be the best.' You need to state how the best will be
  measured and any mitigating factors that will be taken into
  account. The data report on which the rewards will be based
  may need to be named precisely so there is no confusion as to
  what we mean by, for example, 'the monthly report'.

- *Tell them what the rewards are and how many will win them.*
  Some campaign sponsors choose not to tell the participants what
  the rewards are until the programme is under way to create
  an element of surprise. This never works. Participants need to
  know what the deal is before they will commit themselves to
  improving their performance; otherwise participation rates will
  be low. The biggest single communication issue with reward and
  recognition is active uptake. It therefore makes sense to promote
  the rewards as well as you can. No one would advertise a new
  product without saying what it is or does. Details of the rewards

are important in the decision-making process of participants about getting involved, so simply saying there will be 'a holiday' is not enough. Ideally you need to say where the holiday will be, how long it will be, what venue you will be using and what costs are included, especially travel-related costs. Another factor in participants deciding to support the programme will be their perception of their chances of winning. If there are 1,000 potential participants and only one reward most people are unlikely to get very excited about taking part. If you have 'hundreds of awards' then talk about it to get the highest possible take-up.

- *Participants need to know about any hidden catches.* To ensure good communication, put yourself in the shoes of the participant and be critical about any possible misunderstandings, which are everywhere when you write things down and publish them. It may be obvious to you that personal tax liabilities are not included, but for most participants a prize should not come with a tax bill. If participants change job roles halfway through the programme, where do they stand in terms of credits for performance up to that point? If the reward is a holiday but the participant is unable to travel, is it clear what the sponsor will provide as an alternative, if any?

- *The sponsor needs to have a policy in cases of dispute.* It is inevitable with larger schemes that there will be misinterpretation of the rules with regard to who qualifies for which rewards. There should be a clear statement of what the arbitration procedure is and who will have the final say. In some cases there may be a genuine error in data or in the way that the rules were promoted, so sponsors need to have a means to protect themselves from mischievous bending of the rules or in certain circumstances attempts at fraud. It is advisable to have a catch-all clause that states that the programme is non-contractual and can be withdrawn by the organization at any time for whatever reason.

- *Tell them what you are going to say and when.* One of the most common complaints in post-programme research is that participants did not know what documents they were supposed to use to verify the rules and how to find out about ongoing performance. Part of good programme communication is to provide a clear explanation of all the criteria for qualification in a single document and to tell participants that you will be communicating their performance on a regular basis throughout the programme. You may also need to confirm when and how the winners will be informed to avoid ad hoc communication once the campaign has come to a close.

It would be tempting to spend a lot of time drafting formal rules and then getting them checked by legal counsel, if you have one, to be absolutely sure that you have covered everything, but this would be a mistake. It has to be remembered that a reward and recognition programme is a discretionary, participatory project rather than a contract. If there are too many rules and too much legal jargon, participants will just switch off. This is even more true when you are incentivizing business partners.

There is thus a balance to be struck between ensuring that everyone understands the rules of the deal and putting people off participating. It is well worth trialling the copy draft with some members of the key participant groups to get feedback on understanding the offer before confirming the final words and phrasing. You should also get sign-off from the main internal sponsors just in case some technical element has changed since the first time they agreed the basic rules.

The media of programme communication

Now that we have determined the differences between communicating rewards and recognition and decided what the rules are going to be, the remaining decision to be made in communication terms is how.

There is no doubt that the recommended route for most reward and recognition schemes these days is online, but plain text e-mails are not enough. They merge too easily into standard internal messages,

FIGURE 7.1 Model for optimum participant engagement

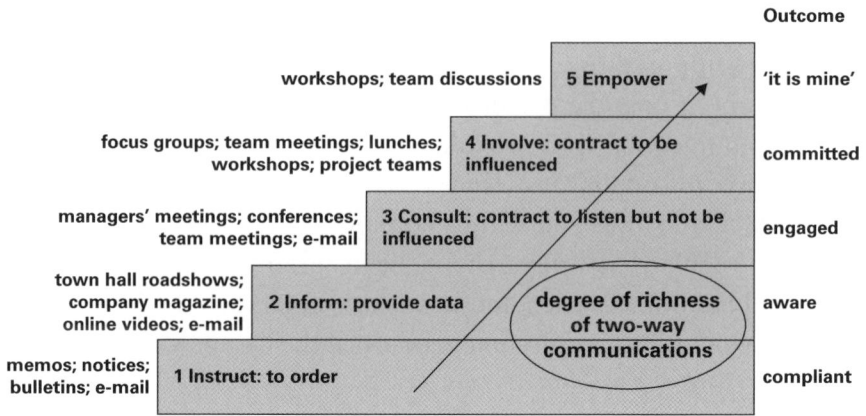

and the main point of reward and recognition programmes is that they should stand out from the crowd and be noticed as something unusual. In my book *Strategic Brand Engagement* (Fisher, 2014: 75) I outline the process of achieving the best possible engagement with employees with any internal message using John Smythe's (2007) model (Figure 7.1).

As you can see on the left-hand side of Figure 7.1 there are a number of media and combinations of media, which rise in effectiveness depending on their usage. The most striking thing about the model is the mix of e-mail, public view and face-to-face media to get the best possible engagement with the message. Each audience needs to be viewed against the potential merits of the suggested combination. Naturally each medium has an associated cost, even if it is simply the work hours it takes to produce it rather than their per-item cost. But, whichever combination of techniques and media is chosen, good initial design and eye-catching visuals are key parts of the process. Simply putting the rules online and adding an organization logo are not enough to make the communication stand out for most participants.

Although current media techniques are dominated by online content, physical boosts to promotion such as wall posters, printed flyers and desktop give-aways being distributed at various times during the campaign can make for an interesting and varied message to create spikes in activity. The best programmes seem to be those that combine creatively an online presence with offline printed items to mix up the message to surprise participants. In terms of communication planning a formal media plan should be drawn up so that the sponsors know what will be produced and by when, as would happen in the planning of a consumer campaign.

Portals

The most common communication model for both internal programmes and business partner schemes is the creation of a dedicated web portal. The advantages are many. Individual security can be provided through access to the intranet as the first gateway. For external business partners a password and personal identity code can be supplied to allow independent participants access to the programme site. Both sites can be cell- or mobile-optimized so that participants can stay connected with their reward or recognition programme when they are away from their desks.

Features of such a portal could include skills videos so that new skills can be learned and practised online without the need for participants to attend expensive training sessions in the main office or in hotel venues. News items and announcements can be made 24/7, which is particularly useful for large organizations that operate across many time zones. Individual updates on personal performance can be posted as soon as they are verified, with corresponding congratulations messages from relevant line managers. Depending on the database capabilities of the site virtually instant assessment of reach, take-up, comments and business analysis can be provided. Getting a clear picture of the effect of the programme no longer needs to wait until the 'wash-up' at the end of the campaign. This means that tweaks to improve the style and detail of the programme can be made on an ongoing basis. A blog section is another helpful addition, with which most participants will be familiar, to exchange best-practice tips and ensure that the site changes its content on a daily basis rather than simply being put up at launch and then largely left unchanged.

With a communication plan under way and a mix of online and offline media being produced to make the programme conspicuous, the final missing piece of the PIP jigsaw is the reward element. There is no single silver bullet when it comes to reward. It all depends on the audience, the performance improvement being asked for and the resources that have been allocated to achieve the required ROI. In Chapter 8 we discuss the potential reward options and the best strategies for deciding what to give to whom and why.

Rewards

08

Performance improvement programmes work best when there is a reward somewhere down the line. Recognition is good practice, but a certificate with no intrinsic value can often be discarded. There has to be something worth making an effort for; otherwise why would most people even bother to become involved? Reward and recognition programmes rely on the optional participation and the good will of individuals. Choice of an appropriate reward will make a bottom-line difference to the success of your programme and get more participants in your scheme than if it has no reward element.

We know from Chapter 2 that incentives work, so not providing rewards for good compliance makes no sense at all. You want the programme to succeed. Having analysed past schemes, done your research, skilled up the participants to make personal changes and planned the communication you now need to consider the most effective reward or incentive for the budget you have set for the campaign.

Before we begin to discuss what rewards may be appropriate for certain types of change in performance we need first to talk about money, specifically why money is not the answer to most motivational issues. In Western society, which is based on the capitalist system, it seems counter-intuitive to suggest that money, and lots of it, does not work as a means to encourage higher performance, but the body of research evidence is so overwhelming that it would be foolish to ignore it all. Above a minimum level, money as an incentive shows diminishing returns. This can be hard to appreciate, as business is hard-wired to measure success in terms of stock price, cash in reserves and annual returns. So let's look at the business case for not simply reaching for the coffers when a reward is needed to change performance.

Does more money produce higher performance?

The main method most organizations use to promote higher performance is more money. The roots of such thinking are embedded in the 19th century, when the highs and lows of demand and manufacturing production meant that employers wanted to pay out only when their overheads were covered. Higher-than-average production meant higher bottom-line profits. The reasoning was that more cost per item would be given away in return for higher productivity. This model works very well when standards of living are low and any additional income can make a tangible difference to workers' lifestyles. But in the 21st century this is no longer the case in the developed world. Relatively few people live in borderline poverty compared with the majority of working people, and the social welfare system of most Western governments means that, should you struggle to make ends meet, there is a safety net to cover most situations. With the introduction of government-led minimum wages policies it is unusual to find employees at the risk of dying of starvation through lack of money.

During the 20th century not only did most business sectors and government departments establish a 'going rate' for most jobs but there was a large increase in the provision of employment-related welfare. We have seen in Chapter 1 that there are many specific advantages of being formally employed. Some commentators report that the value of such benefits can be as much as 30 per cent of total take-home remuneration. For most people in full-time employment in a growing economy the total remuneration package is usually more than enough to create loyalty and commitment to an employer, but weekly or monthly pay cheques do not distinguish between contractual effort and above-average effort. The perception is that whatever effort the employee makes personally in achieving tasks there is no more reward available. Basic pay seems to cover the contractual fulfilment of the job description and no more. This leads in turn to a generally lower level of individual performance than in previous decades. Put simply, why work harder if you do not need to?

Bonuses do exist, of course. It is common practice to be enrolled in an end-of-quarter or end-of-financial-year bonus scheme where employees receive a relatively small reward for their contribution to the overall success of the organization. This is good in theory but in practice it is rather too broad a brush to be an effective motivator. In an organization of say 1,000 people it is virtually impossible to determine the level of each individual's contribution to the overall performance of the organization. A 1 or 2 per cent cash payment at the year end is always welcome, but after taxes and the delay in paying out the bonus there is virtually no perceived link between the individual's activity at work and the payment. This means it does not become habitual as an incentive mechanism, so as an organizational technique to raise performance it becomes inefficient and untrustworthy.

Commission can and does work in some specific situations where the individual has direct control over performance. Typically this will be in a sales or representation network where personal effort is usually directly related to success. All other factors being equal the salesperson who makes the most calls or does the most research into prospects gets the business. In this job context it is clear that offering a basic salary with generous cash commission on top related to specific sales is a good way to generate better performance at the least cost to the organization. However, care needs to be taken to ensure that the basic pay is enough to survive on but not so much that the commission element is perceived not to be necessary. To some extent it could be argued that commission is a throwback to earlier times where the employee contracts willingly to earn a minimal amount because the perceived cash rewards are much greater than could be earned through regular employment of an administrative nature. Most employees require a more predictable income stream than a basic or commission package delivers, so this way of being remunerated does not suit the vast majority of workers.

Performance-related pay

In theory, if you could identify specific performance in a job context then paying more money to those individuals should be motivational, shouldn't it? This is the basis of performance-related pay (PRP) and all its variants such as profit sharing, gainsharing, share ownership, share options, competence pay and many others. But does it actually produce the results?

In 1964 Victor Vroom studied work performance in manufacturing and discovered that once a certain level of economic comfort had been attained offering more money in return for higher productivity actually impaired performance, as it created unproductive stress. The use of such schemes reinforced the workforce's view that management perceived them as simply the means of production, which could be manipulated just like plant and equipment to make higher profits.

A study by Jensen and Murphy (1990) compared the relationship between pay and overall corporate performance. After analysing the performance of over 2,000 executives within some 1,200 different organizations in the United States they concluded that there was no actual correlation between PRP and company performance. In addition they found that 'executives tended to be overpaid for bad performance and underpaid for good performance'.

A follow-up research project by Berlet and Cravens (1991) covering 163 US companies also concluded that the link between executive pay and the organization's performance was virtually random.

In *Unjust Rewards*, Polly Toynbee and David Walker (2009) exposed the myth that PRP creates higher performance from executives. They found that in the United Kingdom PRP by itself not only failed to improve corporate performance but actually led to a downward spiral of demotivation if customer demand was poor. A general view was held that whatever effort you put in could not change a flat market into a buoyant market. In the same way, share options and their many variants tend to disappoint participants because there are many external factors that can trigger major movements in share prices that have no relationship to the personal efforts of individuals.

Money versus massage

In 2004 Scott Jeffrey, assistant professor of management sciences at the University of Waterloo, Ontario, published the results of a small experiment undertaken at the University of Chicago regarding using massage as a reward as an alternative to money. The participants were students, so we can assume that money would be quite an attractive proposition as a reward.

They were asked to take part in a word game on campus in pursuit of an incentive. One group was rewarded with money. The second group qualified for a therapeutic massage of varying length according to their performance. The market value of the rewards was equal. There was a third control group that was not offered any reward. The massage group were then asked whether they would have preferred the cash rather than the massage, and 78 per cent said they would. However, the analysis of relative performance revealed that although the cash group performed 14.6 per cent better than the control group with no incentive the massage group performed 38.6 per cent better than the cash group, over twice as big an improvement.

Further follow-up questions showed that the participants found it difficult to justify spending the equivalent cash on a massage but would be perfectly happy to receive a massage as a reward for specific tasks. This study suggests that overall tangible rewards for employees spent on discretionary aspirational rewards are more effective than cash. The bottom line is that most participants will say in research that all they want is more money, but they actually perform better in reality for non-cash rewards, all other factors being equal.

Self-fulfilling prophecy

If the case for not using money to encourage higher performance and incremental effort is so strong why is it still so prevalent as a management tool in most of the developed world? It may be worth turning to studies of business leaders and entrepreneurs to find some answers. The psychological profile of successful entrepreneurs tends to perpetuate the idea that money or its accumulation is everyone's driving force. If it works for the business leader, why not for the workers? Simply offering more money therefore becomes a self-fulfilling prophecy. Individuals have been subjected to schemes involving more money for higher performance for so long that participants feel it must be what works best; otherwise why would leaders offer it so often as an incentive or reward for higher performance?

Mazda Motor Corporation

What we need is definitive proof from the market that when given a straight choice participants in a commercial environment work harder for non-cash incentives than they do for the cash equivalent, however strange that may appear to be from a logical viewpoint.

When Mazda Motor Corporation was planning an incentive to motivate Mazda car dealers to sell B-Series trucks, Mazda's 900 dealers were sharply divided on what kind of incentive reward would work best to improve sales from their 2,000 sales managers and 6,000 salespeople. Some were adamant that only more money would move the metal from the forecourt. Others favoured non-cash rewards such as gift cards, travel or merchandise. After all the debate was over, a trip to Aspen, Colorado was offered to the top 15 sales managers, but for those who did not qualify for the hosted travel event a compromise was reached. Upper management at Mazda were leaning towards offering money but decided to test the theory that non-cash works better than cash by implementing a straight split in terms of rewards. Half the dealer sales staff were enrolled into a programme where they could earn up to $75 for each unit sale. The other half were offered a multi-level award product called AwardperQs whereby winners could choose their own reward items, depending on their performance. To add to the attractiveness of the incentive, participants were invited to call a toll-free number after each sale to claim a randomly distributed reward, either in cash or in AwardperQs. The rewards ranged between US$10 and US$250. This 'spin-and-win' format is quite common with large incentive programmes, as just one unit sale could result in considerable returns for the participant.

The results of the reward comparison test were astonishing. The non-cash group consistently achieved higher sales levels throughout the campaign period, and this was true regardless of the size of the dealership. At the end of the campaign the cash group had managed only a 2.18 per cent increase over their sales objective, whereas the non-cash group had achieved a 15.65 per cent increase.

Post-campaign qualitative research showed that the low-volume dealers were not enthused by just $75 for every additional truck sold, as they calculated that they would not be able to sell enough volume to make it worthwhile after deductions. However, those in the non-cash group could clearly identify in personal and family terms what the rewards would be and worked towards their goals almost regardless of the equivalent monetary value. Mazda's own post-campaign research concluded: 'A reasonable assumption is that the emotional impact of an offer of tangible rewards such as merchandise or travel is more powerful from a behavioural change point of view than is an offer of an equivalent sum of money' (Mazda, n.d.).

Trophy value

Human motivation is a complex area, as we have already discovered. Although no institution has ever measured the actual difference in performance between those who receive 'recognition' and those who receive reward, experience of life tells us that winning recognition awards can be the spur to higher achievement even though the cost of such recognition is minimal. The common phrase used to describe such kudos is 'trophy value'. In general, individuals do not like to talk about how much they earn or what cash bonus they have received as a result of their efforts at work, but they will talk about receiving letters or e-mails of commendation or being hosted to dinner by their boss or senior management. For many years the lure of incentive group travel as a reward was largely to be able to talk about the exotic destinations winners had been to with their organization as a result of their individual efforts. The fact that most people could not afford to fly halfway around the world and stay in five-star hotels created a trophy value for the award that would remain in the memory for many years in a way that a cash bonus after taxes never would.

A summary of these examples, studies and experience in the real world is that, to foster discretionary, non-contracted improvements in performance, non-cash rewards work better than monetary rewards, despite what people tell you. In truth non-cash rewards can also be perceived as having a higher value than cash, especially if you are buying in bulk or on behalf of a specific sponsor. Discounts can be considerable if your potential winners share a profile that suppliers think they can sell more to after the reward has been presented. We all know that the cost of acquiring a new customer is very high, so sampling a product or service through being an award winner is one way for a reward supplier to expand their marketing database, for which privilege they may reduce their unit cost.

Rewards preferences

In terms of individual items there are naturally hundreds of thousands of options at all kinds of value points from which you could choose to reward high-achieving winners, but the key issues are which type of reward is more effective than other types and how these rewards can be delivered in a prompt and timely manner.

Many surveys have been conducted to try to discover which specific item would deliver higher performance than any other. I once researched this with 4,000 Prudential Insurance salespeople, and the most popular item was an Albert Rose china teapot! In reality there is no such magic item, as it all depends on the choice being offered, the budget and the profile of the winners. During the 2000s Motivcom plc, a British consultancy, canvassed 800 buyers to discover which type of reward would be more favoured than others for use within the context of incentive programmes. As you can see from Table 8.1, most sponsors said 'cash', although we know it is actually the least effective incentive. The most popular non-cash item was group hosted travel, followed by gift cards, then individual items of merchandise and lastly tickets for sporting events. We could interpret this finding in the following way. Group or family holiday rewards have the highest cost per head and arguably deliver the most satisfying life experience, in other words a holiday that you will remember for many years if not for your entire life. Gift cards provide the ultimate choice of reward, as you can decide exactly what you want to be rewarded with, so they are personally highly motivational. Specific items of merchandise are good, but only if you do not already possess the item

TABLE 8.1 Reward preferences

Reward medium	Percentage
Cash	43
Overseas travel	35
Gift cards	23
Tangibles	20
UK breaks	16
Sports events	14

SOURCE Motivcom plc

or service being requested. You can only have so many televisions or iPads. Perhaps surprisingly tickets for sporting events come in last, which can probably be explained by the fact that not everyone likes sport (although many competitive sales managers do) and not everyone likes the same sport.

Apart from the group holiday option where everyone travels together, the key element of the rank order of the other types of reward is the element of choice. It is no surprise that gift cards are the best low-cost incentive reward, because they give the participants what they want as their own personal reward. This does not mean that every programme should offer only gift cards. As we have seen in our discussions about programme structures (see Chapter 4), most effective programmes have several tiers, with each one appealing to a section of the participant audience but all interlocking as part of a single scheme.

Types of non-monetary reward

Let's examine each type of reward in turn and consider which rewards work better for which participant universes and what constraints there may be for each reward category.

Incentive or group travel

At the top of almost everyone's wish-list as a reward is a holiday. This could, of course, be a family holiday if won in the form of gift cards to a specific value from a travel supplier. Some sponsors prefer to reward in this way rather than host a specific holiday or convention, to provide the maximum amount of choice but also to avoid the inevitable central cost in executive time of organizing and hosting a large gathering. However, by incentive travel we mean a single event, hosted by the organization, with invitees having to qualify through achieving specific performance criteria. My definition of incentive travel would be that discipline of sales and marketing and management which uses promise, fulfilment and memory of any exceptional travel-related experience to motivate participating individuals to attain exceptional levels of achievement in their place of work or education.

Group or incentive travel tends to follow a specific pattern, with variations for the duration and purpose of the visit. In essence it is a short holiday packed with experiences and opportunities to celebrate, but the most important aspect is its promotion. Table 8.2 shows a typical promotion schedule that you would expect to see as part of an incentive travel initiative.

Incentive travel is by far the most attractive reward that can be offered by most sponsors within the context of a reward programme. In the eyes of the average participant it has all the qualities of a luxury holiday but without the personal cost. It appeals to all the senses. It offers relaxation from a stressful life. It provides excellent opportunities as a trophy value reward to impress colleagues and relatives as evidence that you are very successful. However, the product itself should not be confused with a retail holiday, as the costs and details of the programme are quite different.

Flight issues

In general incentive travel events are shorter than most of the holiday rotations offered through retail organizations. When providing consumer holidays, operators rely on being able to charter a specific size

TABLE 8.2 Typical incentive travel promotion schedule

October–December	Development, costing, design of materials.
January	Launch at a sales conference, brochure, video, monthly competition bulletin.
March	Teaser from the destination, newsletter promoting hotel.
June	Teaser, mid-year results, newsletter promoting destination, video to support destination message.
October	Teaser, 'Fast Finish double points' promotion, newsletter promoting pro rata qualifiers, draft itinerary.
January	Final results, congratulations bulletin, joining instructions for qualifiers. (Launch of next year's programme.)

of aircraft for several weeks over the popular periods when consumers want to travel. This means they can organize their programme on the ground at the destination around say seven days so that the aircraft going out can bring back last week's group of holidaymakers and fill up the aircraft for the return journey, as otherwise it would simply return to its home hub or destination empty. Any 'empty legs' are costly, because operators get no revenue for that portion of the flight. Buyers who are new to group travel often ask for 'a charter' if the departure times of the scheduled flights do not exactly match their needs for the incentive group, but the cost is high as a result of the empty leg issue, so it only becomes a viable option for a client that has the budget to fund the additional cost.

Departure times can be problematical. Not every destination in the world has scheduled flights to suit the needs of an incentive group. Owing to the home location of the winning participants some of them may require to be overnighted the day before departure if the scheduled flight time is too early in the morning. Equally, if the scheduled flight is say midday, by the time the group has arrived at the destination, had their luggage transferred and checked in they may well have spent the entire day travelling to the destination rather than enjoying the incentive. This puts pressure on sponsors to provide an extra day, which all adds to the per-head cost of the event. At the other end of the day a scheduled departure time of late evening may sound efficient in terms of time spent at the destination, but most hotels require you to check out at lunchtime, so you need to make provision for the participants for the rest of that day with no access to hotel facilities before they fly. A final aspect of departure times is the actual arrival time back home. Depending on the incentive destination chosen, a late-evening flight may result in arriving back home early in the morning of the next day, which is normally a busy commuting time in most conurbations. So, when it comes to scheduled flight times, there is a lot to consider in terms of logistics, cost and the enjoyment of the event for participants that may not be apparent when first looking at published flight times.

Numbers of participants are a key issue when planning group travel. Unlike gift cards and other distributable items, a seat on an aircraft is a finite product. Once the seat has been booked, it is gone. It is not uncommon to want to fly 50 winners and their partners, so 100 people, to a specific destination within a certain time-frame. To buy 100 seats on the same flight can be difficult, as most routes serve business or individual holiday markets and they will have geared up their schedules to match that market. When a sudden request for 100 extra seats is received it is highly likely that there will not be enough seats, so the group will need to be spread over say a 12-hour departure period. This has knock-on effects for the programme, as your planned 'welcome dinner' may have to be staggered over many hours while you wait for the later guests to arrive.

One way to avoid this is to book your group very early, so some six months prior to departure, if possible. But for many airlines this becomes impractical because for security reasons airlines will not take bookings unless you can provide actual names. For most incentive winners you will not know their names until after the programme has finished. This leads to the practice of providing false names for group bookings by agencies and organizers, who then need to pay the charge for amending the booking to the real names at a later date.

Another aspect of group bookings is that on many routes the airline will not want to accept say 100 bookings, as they do not want their regular travellers not to be able to travel on their normal flight. In terms of passenger yield, by taking the booking for 100 seats they are displacing regular passengers who over a 12-month period provide more revenue to the airline than a single group booking.

These issues of cost versus availability versus displacement all add to the unit price of a group fare bearing very little relationship to the price of a seat you could book direct on the internet as an individual. It often comes as quite a shock for corporate organizers when they realize that not only can they not rely on better rates than published for seats to a specific destination but the airline may not even be able to accommodate everyone on the same flight, no matter how early you book.

A final aspect of flight management is proximity of the airport to the destination itself. When you spend a week in any location, you may be relaxed about a journey time of two hours from airport to hotel. For a group incentive that may only be spending two or three days in the destination, two hours at either end of the programme can eat into the ground programme in a significant way. Sometimes the travel time from airport to hotel may mean you need to look at another more convenient destination for the incentive event to run smoothly.

Taking all these factors into account it is clear that trying to book group travel is a specialist task, and not even business travel implants in large organizations cope well with trying to shoe-horn a large group into a process where they are normally booking for individual business travellers. As we will now discover, hotels have the same issues of displacement, which means that flights and hotels have to be looked at simultaneously; otherwise you will not be able to coordinate flight arrival and departure times with what the hotel can offer.

Island destinations can be an issue. Although any global list of incentive destinations will include such resort destinations as Barbados, Mauritius or Bali, air access to islands can be difficult away from the high tourist peaks of season. There may be many fewer flights than you would expect, and in some cases there may not even be a daily flight. For this reason you need to look very critically at island destinations for your group and determine early on if it is actually practical to be able to get your number of winners there within a reasonable time-frame.

It is easier if all your winners are flying from one airport such as London, New York or Sydney. But within Europe your winners may need to access the destination from their own location or country. This means there have to be reasonable flights for independent travellers. It is highly likely they will have to take connecting flights, with the inevitable delays this will cause to their journey time. It will have an effect on your ground arrangements if a significant proportion of your winners are having to fly independently and take connecting flights. This may be even more problematic for the return journey if flights from the destination are few and far between. Experience of group travel suggests that participants tend to be tolerant about the logistics of the journey there, as they are anticipating having a wonderful time, but they can be highly critical of the time it takes to get home. For the organizer of a motivational event, it makes sense to minimize the irritations involved with international travel and, if that means not opting for a destination that is difficult to get to, so be it.

Chartering flights

If you have the money and you want to avoid these logistical issues, chartering an aircraft or series of aircraft may be an option. You can choose what size aircraft to charter, when it departs and when it takes people home again, and to some extent personalize the interior and even the exterior with corporate livery or provide specific types of in-flight entertainment. This may be a useful option to consider if you are running 'back-to-back' groups, in other words when you have such a large group that it makes sense to do the event three times, one after the other, with the first departing group using the aircraft that arrived with the second group to go home on. As the costs can be high you need to have the contract looked at by your legal team, as each supplier tends to have its own specific clauses in case of non-performance, for example because of adverse weather or air traffic control activity.

Hotel issues

Choosing a hotel presents similar challenges to booking airline seats. Every hotel has a commercial choice to make when taking a booking, as the number of rooms for any particular night is finite. The displacement principle applies in the same way as for airline seats. You may think that any hotel would be very keen to take your booking for a large number of rooms over several nights, but this is rarely the case.

Hotels have regular business travellers who pay a profitable rate in the main for regular use of the hotel. Many almost always use that property whenever they are in town on business, so they expect to be able to get a repeat booking when they want it. Established venues also have a number of regular groups that take space every year at around the same time, so these corporate customers also need to be accommodated.

In the example in Table 8.3 of how a group booking displaces individual bookings activity you can see how taking the group booking means the hotel has fewer rooms to offer its individual customers, who may then not rebook when they are next in town, as their business buying habit has been broken.

An important factor when choosing a hotel for incentives is the capacity to entertain large numbers at check-in, for receptions and for plenary sessions where you may want to get everyone together for a briefing or short conference. These elements can be held outside the property, and many organizers do choose to take such events away from the hotel to provide diversity and interest. But there are logistical issues and costs in moving large numbers of people from one location to another, so being able to do such gatherings all in one place makes sense. A venue that has rooms for accommodation but not enough space to hold a drinks party is not a good choice, whatever the price may be.

A further aspect to consider is whether there are any competitive groups booked in the same venue at the same time. For public sector and government organizations this may not be an issue, but for commercial organizations that may wish to hold meetings about internal issues as part of the incentive programme having a competitor just

TABLE 8.3 Hotel rooms displacement, 220-room capacity

Day of week	Sunday	Monday	Tuesday	Wednesday	Thursday	Friday	Saturday
Forecast of rooms sold	171	197	214	214	214	193	183
Group enquiry	–	15	–	–	–	–	–
Displaced passing trade	2	15	15	10	5	2	0	= 47 room nights

down the corridor, in the main conference room or drinking in the bar may be an issue with senior management. Although some hotels may wish to maintain their obligation of confidentiality they should not have any objection to telling you that another organization that competes directly with you in your market is also holding an event at the hotel at the same time. It may well not be an issue, but at least you are informed enough to have a choice rather than the possibly expensive cost of cancelling and relocating to another venue.

Check-in and checkout are the main bottlenecks logistically for groups in hotels. The venue needs to prove that it understands that incentive groups do not behave like business travellers. In the main they all do the same thing at the same time. They breakfast together, they order room service together (having all returned from the same day trip together) and they check in and out together. Reception and other hotel service departments need to be aware that they need contingency plans to deal with this peaking of demand. In terms of banqueting, most groups eat together in a separate area, as it would be impossible for waiting staff to deal with say 100 guests all arriving at the same time for breakfast at 8.15 am hoping to gather in reception by 9 am for departure for the day's events.

Local support

Having successfully dovetailed your flights into your hotel booking, you then need to consider the ground or site programme. No organizer can be expected to know details of every possible world destination, complete with restaurants, cultural activities and hotel choices. For those reasons there exists a wide network of destination management companies (dmcs) that research and keep up to date with travel and logistical details of their local area in much the same way as national tourist offices do for their countries. There is a fee, as they are usually private trading organizations. Some organizers try to do this for themselves by making repeated site visits prior to the group arriving to check on the logistical arrangements, but there is no substitute for local knowledge about restaurants with the experience to handle large group events, notice of road traffic issues, closure policies of government-owned facilities, public or local holidays and, most important of all, being able to pull strings locally in case of unforeseen issues such as delegates losing their passports or even being arrested!

In some destinations where family and personal links are prized over more formal business relationships you may find that booking your venue through the dmc is actually less costly than doing it direct with the venue or through some booking agency. It is common business practice in some locations for there to be different rate cards for overseas buyers than for local buyers, so it is worth taking advantage of these differentials by talking to a dmc before you go ahead and book direct.

Forward planning with destinations

One final strategic thought about incentive or convention travel is having a long-term view about destination choices. Incentive travel for many organizations is an annual event, and so each year various destinations pitch to be considered. Most destinations are chosen from a list of four or five destination ideas for all kinds of reasons, from price to hotel to accessibility and many other criteria. One problem may be that if you choose somewhere very appealing and exotic in year one you will struggle to meet rising expectations in subsequent years. If you are starting out with group travel, it would help the process to meet improving expectations if you choose three or four destinations that have increasing attractiveness. In Table 8.4 you can see how a European group of winners could steadily have their ambitions met by starting off in Paris and ending in Hawaii. In this way you can begin to develop a 'club' concept for winners to aspire to as the programmes progress.

Gift cards

It comes as no surprise that after group travel, which is arguably the best incentive or reward experience, come gift cards or retail vouchers

TABLE 8.4 Incentive destination progression

Year 1	Year 2	Year 3	Year 4
Paris	Monte Carlo	Miami	Hawaii

as the next most popular item for sponsors wishing to motivate their people. The main attractions are their flexibility, individuality and provision of choice, but a key benefit is that they are less expensive than cash when buying in numbers. Each gift card has its own tariff depending on how it is delivered (plastic, digital, paper), but in general you can expect to receive between 5 per cent and say 15 per cent from face value. This is good for the sponsor as the buyer but equally good for winners, as the face value allows them to buy in store or online at retail prices including any discounts offered.

One of the basic tenets of effective motivation is to provide the reward as close as possible to the time of achieving the objective to reinforce the action and so have it repeated out of habit. Even with the most well-organized incentive travel groups the event is unlikely to happen immediately after the end of the programme. In some circumstances it could be as long as three or four months by the time the winners have been confirmed and all the participants have been invited. Gift cards can now be issued within days of the end of the scheme and even topped up electronically on an ongoing basis if the incentive or reward campaign is a regular offer with no end date.

For some profiles of worker it may be appropriate to tailor the type of gift card to their specific lifestyle. It is possible to buy gift cards from retailers that most closely suit the profile of the potential winners. For example, there seems little point in offering upmarket department store gift cards for part-time telemarketing employees who rarely visit such a store. Equally, Harrods gift cards may be perfect for a team from a high-net-worth individuals' recruiting consultancy based in London. An alternative approach is to choose gift cards that provide significant cash substitute opportunities if the participants' basic remuneration is low. Gift cards for petrol stations, supermarkets and utilities make sense for those who may struggle to pay the bills at the end of the month and would be motivated to have their basic costs dealt with through an incentive programme.

Some sponsors would rather not promote the activities of their closest rivals, so purchasing gift cards from specifically chosen retailers means they can avoid their winners having to redeem their rewards in the retail outlets of their closest rivals.

Universal gift cards

In many markets there are hybrid gift cards that cover many retailers on a single card. The advantage is that participants do not need to seek out specific retail chains to redeem their rewards. The retailers that are signed up to the cards tend to cover all profiles of potential participants, so they are applicable to most employee groups. For some clients universal gift cards can cause issues, as it is not possible to unbundle specific retailers if the client does not want to be promoting competitors' products and services. In such cases you just need to be aware of what the cards can be redeemed for and whether you can accept that sometimes winners will be buying from your rivals when they redeem their credits.

Discount or spend-to-get cards

In some countries volume discounts for many products and services have been negotiated from suppliers in return for access to affinity groups such as members of an association or the employees of a large organization. Typical examples include healthcare and fitness aids. They are often seen in the guise of employee benefits as an addition to the standard remuneration package. We have already discussed in Chapter 1 why benefits do not improve individual performance at work, but the benefits themselves are often mistaken for incentive rewards. In real terms they are an alternative to salary and as a result can be viewed as 'salary sacrifice' items rather than incentive rewards.

Another type of benefit that looks like an incentive product but is not is a discount card. Typically they give access to merchandise that if purchased online via the sponsor's arrangement will result in a small discount from the retail price. If a participant were to spend a week's wages in this way on household products and services the savings would be considerable, but the drawback is that participants need to spend the money first out of income to receive the discount. Like affinity group discounts they have the appearance of being an incentive, but because participants need to spend first to receive the benefit they fall outside the category of unencumbered rewards.

One of the central ideas about incentive rewards, which we have seen in the definition of incentive travel earlier in this chapter, is that the rewards should be aspirational and lifestyle-based rather than merely a replacement for remuneration; otherwise the items have no trophy value and will not be discussed among peers to further promote the incentive programme. This aspect must be carefully considered if you embark on offering specific merchandise, or tangibles as they are sometimes known, as the reward for certain improvements in performance.

Merchandise and tangibles

Before Amazon and the internet, printed merchandise catalogues were the default mechanism for programme rewards. Almost all such catalogues have moved online these days, so the merits or otherwise of printed, hard-copy reward catalogues have been consigned to history. That said, there may be a place for offering specific items of merchandise to keep the rewards within an overall theme.

I devised a travel-themed programme for a household goods retailer in 2013 called 'Going Places'. The owners of the retail outlets could compete for a hosted travel event in Miami. The local store managers could qualify for family holiday gift cards up to a certain amount. Store salespeople competed for a 12-month VIP airline lounge pass (these participants were frequent holiday travellers within Europe). There were instant rewards for anyone in the store who claimed to sell a specific outdoor item with a leisure theme, such as garden furniture, barbecues and camping equipment. To be able to provide these rewards at short notice during the campaign period we had to procure the items in bulk before the programme started and store them centrally, awaiting delivery to the winners to reinforce their activity. There was a discount for buying in bulk, but the sponsor took the risk that we would have some left over at the end of the campaign.

Nowadays, because many merchandise items can be ordered online and delivered within a short time-frame, often overnight, there is little need to have merchandise stored in a warehouse purely for the purposes of fulfilling incentive programmes. The truth is that many suppliers were able to mark up such goods considerably in the past, as sourcing such items and having them available in bulk was a specialist business sector. But with the transparency of the internet and improved delivery infrastructure there is no real need to be choosing from a closed or restricted list of goods.

From time to time there may be logic in sourcing specific novelty or brand-new product items in bulk to support a major incentive, but online catalogues now provide such a wide range of tangibles, gift cards and reward services that having it all printed up is both expensive and time-consuming, with the result that by the time any such catalogue is printed the items may well no longer be available.

Social gifting and charitable donations

As many rewards will by necessity be relatively low-value, some participants appreciate the facility to donate their credits or rewards to others on the basis that they were an unexpected bonus and not central to their monthly income. The ease with which 'points' can be converted into a variety of types of reward means that those rewards can also be gifted to others. It may be that some participants would like to use their rewards as gifts for others, so they may well want to offer those rewards to colleagues or family members as tributes for anniversaries, birthdays or other kinds of celebration.

For others the facility to gift their rewards to a chosen charity can be highly valued and provide a way for participants to 'give back' to their chosen good causes. Mechanisms exist online to make this a standard redemption routine, which appeals to a certain type of participant or could be used in conjunction with an organization-wide initiative at certain times of the year such as Christmas or perhaps an emergency or disasters appeal that catches the imagination of the general public.

Sporting and entertainment tickets

If we return to the theme that programme rewards need to be aspirational or discretionary to the extent that they are sought after, tickets to sporting and entertainment events can be useful reward options. The provision of tickets for major sporting or social events is an industry in its own right in developed markets. In other parts of the world it may be specific individuals within various sporting associations who can provide access to hospitality tickets. Whichever route you need to go down there are some specific issues to do with such tickets that the programme sponsor needs to be aware of.

Just like hotel rooms, tickets for prestigious events are in limited supply, so the economics of the market are that you usually have to pay the full amount up front and it cannot be refunded. This may be a non-starter for some schemes where you may not know how many winners you will have or whether they all want to go to see a particular sporting event.

Owing to the attractiveness and media profile of some global events such as the Olympics, the tickets come with varying levels of hospitality and may have to be purchased in multiples rather than in singles. In some cases you may have to buy tickets for the less well-known events in order to buy the higher-profile activities. This usually means a considerable outlay, which many sponsors feel is not justified for their ROI of a particular performance improvement programme.

The logistics of getting your winners there and back for the event can be problematic, as the event sponsor has probably bought up all the VIP accommodation beforehand, so you will need to budget for paying a premium price if the intention is that your winners stay overnight locally. For the Monaco Grand Prix, for example, almost all the quality tickets for the Sunday race include at least three nights' accommodation in Nice, whether you need them or not. So you will need to have deep pockets and be flexible about the package that surrounds any particular ticket being offered.

If your entertainment event, such as a pop concert, is based on your winning group enjoying the experience together, you need to check that the entry tickets supplied are all in the same area or seating row. Some ticket operators acquire single tickets in various parts of the auditorium, as they are cheaper to acquire than group packages, and sell them on to unsuspecting buyers without telling them that they are not all in the same part of the stadium or venue. Such is the demand for tickets to world-class entertainers such as the Rolling Stones or Madonna that such details get lost in the small print of the contract and only come to light when the actual printed tickets are distributed.

Tailored events as rewards

We have already discussed incentive travel as an overseas tailored reward, but this can be done nationally or locally with a variety of venues and activities that are both enjoyable and aspirational. Local events tend not to need overnight accommodation, so logistically they are simpler to organize. As for most event ideas, the content needs to be tailored to the audience. Shooting clays or going bowling will certainly appeal to many people, but just because the activity is relatively inexpensive or nearby does not mean participants will want to attend and more importantly want to work harder to win a place to attend. Each reward needs to suit as many potential winners as possible in an aspirational way that gets people talking and competing. The biggest failing in most reward campaigns is lack of take-up and engagement. Although communication of the programme is the key element to get right, choice of reward is almost as important and should not be agreed without considerable thought about its appropriateness for the specific participants and the likely success of its delivery.

Balancing rewards

Reward budgets are not infinite, as all reward and recognition programmes need to adhere to an ROI format, but there is considerable scope to mix and match rewards to suit all the potential audiences. The value of individual reward items also makes a difference in terms of getting a balance between their attractiveness and the number of rewards you can afford to offer within the budget. It would be perfect to have everyone fly down to Rio if they hit their performance target, but the costs would be prohibitive. On the other hand everyone could receive varying amounts of credits on their gift cards, but would this be motivational for everyone?

In Chapter 9 we discuss what organizational recognition is and what strategic issues you are likely to face when embarking on the planning of introducing such a programme as a completely new concept into an organization or replacing an old system of recognition that is no longer fit for purpose. Recognition has many links with formal engagement and its measurement. My book *Strategic Brand Engagement* (Fisher, 2014) covers the topic of organizational engagement in much more detail but, for those who wish to know purely how recognition techniques can be applied, please read on.

Recognition

09

It has been said many times by industry recognition practitioners that there should be no reward without recognition and no recognition without reward. In the quest to motivate participants to improve performance, asking people to work harder for no reward is unlikely to be a message they will take to heart. Equally, distributing rewards without conferring recognition for doing a good job is a wasted opportunity by the sponsor to take the credit. We already know from our knowledge of human motivation that people crave recognition and being noticed in almost all life situations, so why not take advantage of this human tendency for the good of the organization?

But what does a practical recognition programme look like in the modern world and what expectations do participants have now that differ from those of say 20 years ago when formal or even informal recognition in organizations was evidenced by little more than a clock when you retired and a faded 'employee of the month' chart on the wall in the works canteen?

Discretionary recognition tends to come in one of four formats within most organizations:

- formal recognition from the executive for specific teams and individuals, usually on a monthly or annual basis;
- peer-to-peer recognition, thanking colleagues for support;
- ideas or suggestion schemes to save or make more money;
- long-service awards.

The internet has changed the way such programmes are now organized in that the intranet provides an opportunity to put individuals in contact with each other in a much more efficient way than before. Let's look at formal recognition by organizational executives, which was the traditional technique to congratulate high achievers and remains prevalent in some industry sectors.

Formal recognition programmes

Traditionally formal recognition schemes have been the poor relation of whatever was produced for the sales or distribution teams. This was mainly due to the fact that incentive programmes are normally paid for from the margins produced from additional sales. Recognition programmes do not produce immediately identifiable returns. They tend to be part of a suite of initiatives undertaken to raise engagement levels and so tend not to stand alone as a 'do this–get that' exercise. Sales incentives tend to be organized by the sales or marketing communications teams, who are well versed in promotional techniques and copywriting that sells concepts. Recognition initiatives are usually handled within the HR team, who are less adept at this kind of communication and often do not have the creative resources to make the output attractive and compelling to read. Without the general carrot of having expensive rewards to promote, HR announcements tend to be less well produced. The result of this syndrome is that formal organizational recognition schemes can be perceived as somewhat stilted and lacking in imagination.

What do formal recognition programmes look like? Most systems have a monthly or quarterly element to recognize exceptional performance in the workplace publicly. It often encourages teamwork, as individual effort is relatively difficult to track for staff with no clear output. Where individual acknowledgement exists it is largely through nomination by line managers and at a fairly low level. Typically this is seen as an 'employee of the month' league table, particularly within retail outlets. Often there is no reward, simply the kudos of being nominated as the standout worker of the period.

The same system can be used on a supervisor level, where supervisors may be nominated within their geographical area or zone as having done an exceptional job. Depending on the size and hierarchy of the organization there may come a point when nominating a senior executive for having done a good job would seem to be open to abuse as the pool of nominators grows ever smaller. In addition, the higher up the ladder the nominees are the more likely they will be benefiting from some kind of key performance indicator system on a regular basis, so there is no real need to be promoting individual performance in a discretionary way.

As the year progresses it is easy to see how 'employee of the month' can become 'employee of the quarter' and eventually 'employee of the year'. Annual programmes are often devised to provide an ongoing impetus to keep impressing your supervisor towards an end goal. Annual schemes usually have nominal rewards such as a celebratory lunch, an amount, but not too much, in gift cards and probably a commemorative certificate for public display. A common promotional device is the production of wearable pins that nominated employees can earn and wear in the workplace. Throughout the 1970s to the 2000s it was normal for financial services organizations to recognize sales performance through the gifting of gold, silver or bronze pins so that aspiring colleagues could see immediately who were the best performers in the organization. The technique was a device borrowed from restaurant chains and retail outlets in the United States, where highly nominated or long-serving employees had the right to wear specific pins or badges to show their achievement. In time this was extended to cufflinks, ties, belts, brooches, scarves and any other kind of wearable so that the winning individuals could be seen to be winners by others as they went about their everyday job. Such displays of formal recognition do not go unnoticed by customers either, so promoting the achievement can be as important as the effect the items have on other employees. In some schemes small jewels were inserted into the wearable to denote how many times the employee had been nominated or how long the employee's service record was. Most nominated employees would be happy to explain to any curious customer what the wearable was for and what had to be done to win one.

The wearing of visible items to denote personal excellence can be a cultural issue in some markets. In the developed West most organizations would expect employees to want to wear recognition pins, and mostly they do. But in some other cultures such adornments may not be welcomed either by the employee or by customers if the employee is in a front-facing role. You may need to be sensitive to cultural norms when suggesting and then imposing such systems on unsuspecting workers.

The involvement of senior relevant executives at an end-of-year celebratory lunch, dinner or off-site event is an important element in raising the profile of the programme without spending large amounts of money or resources. The celebration is then publicized internally to the entire workforce so that other people are reminded that the programme exists and that senior members of staff are involved and fully endorse the programme. If you are an international organization it is relatively simple to construct an additional element of overseas travel, with the national or divisional winners travelling to a global recognition event. This adds to the attraction of getting involved if participants are aware they may get a hosted travel event as a result of doing their best. The only issue to be aware of is that the reward needs to be appropriate to the level of employee and the effort involved in winning or being nominated.

If there is no obvious way to measure support staff performance, how can you ensure that those who are not nominated are still attracted by the programme? The standard way of doing this is to set up a cross-functional committee that meets on a regular basis to put the nominees in rank order and explain their reasoning for choosing certain individuals over others. There may also be some relevant process activities that may have a bearing on individual performance during a specific period. For example, for many organizations pre-Christmas can be an exceptionally busy period, so productivity levels will rise in say the warehouse but not so much in the legal department. There need to be some checks and balances to ensure that it is not always those who deal with numbers, volume or the main customers who are the ones to be nominated.

Another factor to bear in mind is the status of the individual in terms of length of service or any disciplinary procedures that may be ongoing. Although the programme needs to be seen as fair and open to all it may not be very motivational for those who do not qualify to see a short-term intern or someone who is undergoing disciplinary procedures being nominated for an award. It makes sense to have a sense check of who this month's or this quarter's winners actually are, rather than simply produce a rank-order listing from a file and simply rubber-stamp it.

Some organizations take formal recognition so seriously that they are prepared to spend a substantial budget to support their programmes. It is not unusual for call administration organizations, for example, to pay for a 'team of the year' overseas trip for those who consistently perform above the average. Monthly winners often qualify for the competition to win the end-of-year travel event by being assessed against all the monthly winners during the year. An overseas destination can be a powerful incentive to become involved and is highly promotable, so the cost should be viewed as part of the annual scheme rather than a discretionary excess, simply because it is the end of the year.

In summary, formal recognition schemes do a good job at minimal cost by tapping into the latent human desire to be appreciated. The technical issues of how to assess non-sales employees objectively and how to provide meaningful rewards are two reasons why many such programmes are not well promoted and as a result not well regarded by employees who may be fully aware that the sales team receive much higher levels of reward and recognition than they do. Even if the reasons are explained in a commercial way, it still leaves the impression that support teams are less important to the organization than salespeople. This is clearly untrue, but the perception is often the reality.

The overriding characteristic of formal programmes is that they are top-down. They are normally imposed on the employees by the senior management team at minimal cost. The general lack of promotion or integration with overall organizational values tends to result in such schemes being poorly supported internally, especially if there is no reward element, and badly promoted, as other issues crowd in on the senior team. The solution is to try to fix the problems of aligning the programme with the business plan and providing meaningful rewards that reinforce above-average performance.

Peer-to-peer recognition schemes

The opposite of a top-down programme is one that has been discussed with those who will be participating in it. If the process starts with an open discussion the scheme is usually positively endorsed by the potential participants as a useful tool for remembering what the values of the organization are and how they can be applied in everyday work situations. What differentiates peer-to-peer programmes is that employees nominate each other for recognition during the year for everyday demonstrations of corporate values behaviour. It is not difficult to imagine how such a system could be hard to police so that collusion is kept to a minimum and the recognition and rewards process is fair and seen to be fair.

The key to an effective peer-to-peer scheme is the internet. Although many may be aware of paper-based nomination schemes, such schemes were very cumbersome and time-consuming for HR departments and as a result tended to be put at the bottom of the pile of tasks to be completed each month. The consequence was that once launched such schemes tended to receive less promotion and communication than other more pressing issues and quickly faded into the background. With the advent of intranets the promotion and administration of such schemes are now largely automatic, making peer-to-peer programmes much more effective both for the users and for the administrators who need to analyse the data and refresh the messages.

How do they work?

A software package can be created or leased under licence that manages the promotion and nomination of participants. Once loaded up it carries a complete database of all employees and other invited guests such as distributors who are eligible to take part in the programme. Each group of employees is also listed so that specific messages or interaction with those groups can be undertaken, if required.

The first issue to decide is what to measure. We have already mentioned the fact that support employees are difficult to measure in terms of performance, as they have no obvious objective output. Most organizations measure the performance of their support staff in a subjective way through regular appraisals and coaching, but as these meetings are usually once or twice a year they are not very useful as measurements in an ongoing reward or recognition scheme. You need an activity that can be measured on an almost daily basis and that contributes in a meaningful way to the aims of the organization. Organizational values fit very clearly into the category of measurable activities, as the strategy of the organization would be well served if most of the employees carried out their everyday tasks while considering what the organizational strategy was. Typically sponsors choose between four and six values to use as the measurement of 'success'.

Everyone in the programme is given a fixed number of votes they can make, online, each month or period. To avoid cronyism, most schemes allow people to nominate only those on the same level as themselves or lower. Beside each nomination the nominator indicates which of the organization's values the person is being nominated for. It may be that you want to nominate a team that has demonstrated a value. There will be a drop-down box with all the organization's teams already loaded so you can choose the relevant team to reward. It is also possible with some programs to create a specific team to thank from a master list of employees, such as an ad hoc team created for an event or a project.

As soon as people are nominated they receive a communication online saying they have been nominated, which is then added to the database to show a personal tally of nominations for individuals and their position in a rank-order table of potential people to be recognized formally, if that is relevant. They may earn a token payment in gift card credits for being nominated, which is then also held as a credit for immediate or later redemption. At the end of the period the winners are declared and invited to celebratory events, as described in the 'Formal recognition programmes' section above. There may also be a recognition certificate or other trophy for the divisional or national winners.

Deciding on values

The aim of any recognition scheme is to support the organization's strategy. The strategic issue is that most organizational plans are not written to be read by junior members of staff, so the plan needs to be rewritten to take into account the experience and organizational knowledge of those who receive the message. A good example of this is from LV, the UK insurer, which had a major corporate reorganization in terms of how they present themselves to their team and the wider public. Part of this task was to create some values that their core staff could both understand and implement in the ordinary transaction of their business. They settled on four core values:

- Know your stuff (emphasis on product knowledge and personal development).
- Don't wait to be asked (encouraging initiative and problem solving).
- Make it feel special (customer focus and team leadership).
- Treat people like family (being supportive, helpful and friendly).

It is clear from this example that the organization has tried very hard to ensure that the values are obvious and show how ordinary employees can become involved in the strategy by being recognized for seeking out opportunities to display the required performance in the workplace, not only to their supervisors but to their peers as well.

It is possible that over time other strategic priorities come to the fore and existing ones disappear, once learned, so the system should be flexible enough to be able to promote and communicate changing values as the programme is refreshed each year. Ideally when the programme is reviewed some analysis of the back-end data can be done to determine what proportion of the participants were rewarded under which values. Some discussion needs to be had if, say, one of the values is rarely chosen for a nomination. It means either that the value is so well ingrained that no emphasis is required or that it is irrelevant in the current business climate. It will also highlight to supervisors if specific teams have been neglecting certain aspects of the organizational mission and that those aspects need to be played up or rebriefed into the relevant town hall meetings.

Ideas and suggestion schemes

Suggestion schemes for employees have existed ever since the Industrial Revolution of the 18th century. Who better to ask for advice about improving the organization's performance than your own people?

Pre-internet, such programmes had become rather tired, difficult to administrate and of dubious value to the organization in the final analysis. The time taken to evaluate hundreds of ideas from a large organization, many of which had a similar theme, such as improving hygiene factors for employees, submitted on paper, presented most internal departments with a difficult choice: don't ask for ideas and miss out on the opportunity to discover a huge saving on costs; or ask people for their suggestions for improvement but then allocate valuable resource to sifting out the useful ideas from those that simply cost more money and provide no benefit to the organization. Intranet technology has changed the way such schemes can be administered. Apart from the initial set-up the administration is now minimal, so asking employees about how things could be improved or what they think about specific processes is back in fashion.

The starting point for ideas schemes is what benefit they bring, because although administration costs are much lower than they used to be there is still an associated cost in devising the online programme, promoting the scheme on a regular basis and offering a tiered reward system, however token those rewards may be.

ROI for ideas schemes

The concentration on actual returns from employee programmes has resulted in much more emphasis on the business or organizational benefits of 'nice-to-have' schemes. Ideas schemes of any type offer a clear return on investment in most cases, but they are more effective if they emphasize two types of criteria for new ideas: saving costs; and creating new revenue streams.

When Lucent Technologies in the United States introduced an ideas programme for all their staff they called it 'It's All About ME'. ME is the acronym for the microelectronics division. The scheme was devised to improve employee engagement through asking for and rewarding any ideas that either saved costs or created new or improved revenue streams. Participants received points for submitting workable suggestions to achieve either of these two objectives. During the course of the scheme over 54 per cent of the employees took part and submitted something. There were 6,000 ideas collected, of which 2,100 were implemented, in such areas as recycling scrap, reducing the cost of overnight mail, improving plant safety and making e-mail more efficient. During the first year of the programme £13 million (US$20 million) was gained through cost savings and revenue generation at a cost of under £1 million (US$1.65 million). In terms of rewards, employees earned points for any ideas submitted, which could be redeemed for a variety of gifts. For the larger process savings, cash rewards were offered depending on the strategic value of the ideas.

One of the issues with ideas schemes is the administration of 'open suggestions'. If the idea is simply to fix some process that is going wrong then a simple e-mail or technical briefing is easy to implement and, once the new way of doing things has been learned, everyone can adopt it. As with the Lucent Technologies example, simply changing the organization's policy about sending mail may be all that is required to make considerable cost savings. But broader suggestions may need to be investigated by specialist departments such as finance or legal before they can be implemented. It can take several months and require several iterations before a suggestion can be implemented as a genuinely new idea. Using the intranet the same software system could be used to distribute the new idea, form a group to examine it, schedule an expert committee to review it and then even test it before it goes live to all concerned. The technique with intranet-based ideas schemes is to cut down on time-consuming and difficult-to-schedule internal assessment meetings by doing most of the discussion online and meeting together only at critical decision-making points.

Reward strategy for recognition programmes

It is intuitive that employees who offer up ideas to save the organization money should be rewarded for their efforts but, if you offer too little, participants may feel cheated and will disengage from the process. If you offer too much, employees may spend more time thinking up new ideas than actually doing their job. There is a balance to be struck between offering too little and too much. You should also consider whether there should be encouragement to get involved in the first place, whether a particular idea is adopted or not.

In many programmes the crucial metric is the number of participants who engage with the process. To encourage submission of ideas and suggestions those who submit ideas that are on brief and reasonable are rewarded with a token credit worth perhaps the equivalent of a cup of coffee (in some markets the rewards could actually be coffee shop credits!). Although experience shows that most of the ideas submitted will not be taken forward for a variety of reasons the act of submission and having the ideas evaluated all helps the viral message that it is a positive experience and so will be repeated. So some element of the rewards budget should be set aside for this aspect.

It may be worth considering stepped rewards for ideas that reach a second or a third evaluation stage on the basis that the more seriously the idea is evaluated the more merit it has. This structure also incorporates the notion that individuals may have a dozen or more ideas in play at any time so they will return to the recognition site on a regular basis to see how their ideas are progressing. If this is the reality of your scheme then perhaps a tiered system of rewards may be appropriate for people who submit say more than five ideas in any period or are the most prolific ideas generators in their category or division. There are many ways to cut the reward cake to encourage active and ongoing engagement with the programme.

Organizations often struggle with the concept of paying out large rewards to employees, even if the idea has resulted in significant savings or incremental revenues. A saving of 1 per cent on a process improvement for a large organization could run into the hundreds of thousands in reward in theory. For this reason most schemes put a cap on the most you can earn from any single idea. However, the recognition element may be stepped up in the form of national recognition by senior executives and perhaps a paid-for family holiday. In some countries there are national suggestion scheme associations that run national competitions to recognize the best use of such schemes and sometimes the best ideas, as judged annually by a panel of industry experts. This could provide even more reasons for someone who has a skill in coming up with process improvements to continue to contribute even if they have exhausted the recognition and reward system within their own organization.

A further advantage of putting such a programme online with an attached database is the facility to search the database of ideas so as not to pursue an idea that has already been submitted. This not only wastes the time of the assessors but frustrates participants who may spend many weeks honing their idea only to find someone else has already submitted the same or a similar improvement. On the positive side, simply reviewing other people's suggestions can provide material to adapt and amend processes to suit new areas. Collaboration is a key part of online ideas schemes, so this element should be encouraged through shared social media and internal blogs. This was not possible with the old-style, paper-based systems.

The strategic question about rewards within recognition schemes is that the reward should not be pitched so high that it becomes an end in itself. Such programmes are not designed to be cash substitutes or an alternative to the salesforce commission scheme. The amounts offered should not be life-changing or distract attention from the everyday tasks of employees. If you wanted to have a rule for rewards you could say that at the basic level an employee should not be able to earn more than say 0.5 per cent of salary through the recognition programme. At the top end, in terms of national or divisional rewards, they should not exceed say 5 per cent of average salary and should never be paid out in cash, for all the reasons we have discussed in Chapter 8.

Another conundrum will be whether to allow senior-level executives to be rewarded under the scheme. Owing to their experience and expert knowledge of their market sector and the way that organizations function best they will have plenty of ideas about how things should be improved, but that would be part of their job description in most cases. It would be a little difficult to justify were they to earn an additional bonus, even if it were non-cash, for ideas that they should be putting forward anyway. If they are not active participants in the scheme, they still need to be involved by encouraging employees to submit ideas, assessing ideas online and serving on high-level committees where the more important ideas are discussed and perhaps adjusted to fit the organization. They need to be seen to be involved; otherwise their direct reports will perceive that this is a programme the senior-level executives do not value and so will not participate themselves.

The strategic outcome of ideas and suggestion schemes is two-fold. First and overall it is to provide an engagement opportunity for individuals to think about the processes with which they are involved and improve on them rather than wait for an enlightened supervisor or manager to come up with improvements. In theory the best people to see what is going wrong are those who actually do the job every day. The second benefit is the discovery of a major saving that could run into the millions if adopted over several years and across all the business units. We discussed earlier in the chapter the implementation by Lucent Technologies of 2,100 ideas in the space of one year. From this impressive list it is likely that there were no more than say 10 suggestions that had a major impact on costs and probably only five that were ongoing savings rather than one-off advantages. But those five ideas were worth the administration cost of generating the many hundreds of less effective ideas.

In summary, ideas schemes, when done professionally with due regard to regular communication and tweaking of the messages, produce many times the benefits compared to the costs. In the Lucent Technologies example there was a return of 13 times the cost of the set-up and rewards. Although the technique has suffered in recent years as being somewhat old-fashioned there is no doubt that if organized efficiently it is a net contributor to most organizations, sometimes astonishingly so.

Long-service awards

It is right to classify long-service awards as part of the traditional suite of recognition techniques that any organization can use. They can be a retention device for those who remain employed for long periods and an expression of organizational values to those who remain when someone retires. The two benefits to the organization need to be separated though, as the goals of each technique are not the same, even though they are normally promoted as being part of the same package, so to speak.

Periodic recognition for long service

Many mature organizations run some kind of long-service rewards programme, particularly within the manufacturing sector where employees tend to stay longer in their employment than in many other sectors. It is unlikely there has ever been any research into the effectiveness or ROI of long-service awards apart from who spends what, the range of gifts offered and how the schemes are structured. Pre-internet, many large organizations ran long-service programmes as a given without much questioning as to what they were for.

Within established organizations, perhaps with members of the same extended family working for one employer for several generations, there would have been a constant need to acknowledge the contribution of long-serving individuals by means of a formal announcement, a certificate and sometimes an ex gratia gift. In most Western economies this idea is enshrined in legislation, as recipients receive tax concessions up to certain limits for long-service awards. Merchandise suppliers that were keen to make profits out of this phenomenon started to produce printed catalogues of 'suitable gifts' and virtually invented the market for long-service awards, which until then had been handled in a relatively informal manner.

The original concept presupposes that employees stay a long time with the same employer. The Bureau of Labor Statistics in the United States (2014) puts the average length of tenure as follows: 'The median number of years that wage and salary workers had been with their current employer was 4.6 years in January 2014, unchanged from January 2012.' Some recent surveys show that those who are now in their 20s experience a decline in their income if they choose to stay with their current employer for more than two years. There is economic pressure for relatively new recruits to move on from their first employer if they can. If you look at the number of employees who actually qualify for long-service awards it is clear that the numbers are reducing dramatically. Dealing with 'long-term' employee awards has become a thing of the past for most HR departments to the extent that the number of employees who achieve 20 or 30 years' service is relatively insignificant. This suggests that the concept of being obliged to provide long-service awards no longer exists. The idea of a long-service award can then become a retention device strategically set at five years or so.

How to deal with long-service awards

The best way of looking at long service is to create an accurate analysis of your current workforce and work back from there. There is no point in devising a complex award process if you have only three people who could possibly qualify. The system would be based on trigger points for people who resign and join a competitor or another employer. The received wisdom is that awards should be set at say 10, 15, 20 and 25 years of service. This is probably not the workforce of most organizations, especially those with a younger profile. Depending on your analysis it may be that you find your pattern of exits is three, five, seven and then 15 and 20 years. What this is telling you is that in this particular example the first seven years are crucial in retaining staff. In this case you need to be establishing ways to recognize and engage with employees in their early years, not their later years. Instead of long-service awards most employers should be thinking of continued-service awards and recognizing employees for achieving longer-than-average employment periods rather than an arbitrary 20 or 25 years. Possibly a phrase such as 'commitment awards' would set a better expectation for what such awards are supposed to achieve.

In terms of when rewards should be offered, if the crucial point of potential exit is seven years this suggests that the recipient is under 30 years of age, so a clock or similarly unimaginative gift is clearly both thoughtless and possibly insulting. It would be much better to offer age-appropriate rewards and preferably digitally delivered, as this fits with the average profile of an employee under 30. There is no problem with the formal gathering, a lunch perhaps and a talk by someone who takes senior responsibility for that work group, as this is all consistent with human recognition theory.

The organization needs to be seen to be making a personal effort to say 'Well done' to these loyal workers. For busy working managers such events may be seen as chores to be added to the already heavy list of tasks, but in terms of continued loyalty and retention attendance at such events not only is beneficial to the organization but demonstrates core values of employee commitment and teamwork, which are easily eroded if such opportunities to be seen to be acknowledging long service (however short in absolute terms) are not taken.

Retirement gifts

The digital revolution means that there is no longer a need to purchase specific gifts, as retirees can choose what they want from an online selection. Best practice though is to make time for the retiree to choose the item beforehand so that it can be presented as an actual reward at the formal session, even if it is just holiday gift cards. This subtlety shows that you are taking the event seriously and that there has been some prior planning. From an organizational viewpoint the purpose of rewarding retirees is to promote the values of the organization as a caring employer to those who are still employed and therefore promote more loyalty. The link is tenuous in ROI terms, but it is surprising how positively employees can respond when the organization takes time to acknowledge past contributions when strictly speaking it does not have to.

The changes in legislation across Western Europe and the rest of the developed world with regard to 'official' retirement ages and the change in what retirement income schemes can be afforded by the state have meant that it is not simple to work out who is actually retiring. If you add to this decision tree that it may be illegal in some jurisdictions even to require employees to retire at a certain age, notifying employees that they are eligible for an award may be problematic. Database management is key to avoiding embarrassing announcements, so it is worth spending some time looking at long-service awards in general and getting agreement to the principles rather than simply run off a spreadsheet and hope for the best.

Recognition is often viewed as a soft issue when it comes to employee engagement. This is far from true. If you run a peer-to-peer programme you can measure the improvement in engagement and hence the additional bottom-line effect of the percentage increase.

Ideas schemes are equally accountable and should be viewed in terms of the value of the ideas generated. Long service is less straightforward in terms of ROI but, if you view long service as a means to improve retention, improvement in holding on to effective employees can also be measured. The days of retiring on a specific date are long gone, so motivation professionals need to find ways to make the most of such programmes to ensure that the suite of recognition schemes are consistent with organizational values and with each other so that employees can see that the organization is speaking with one voice rather than running a motley collection of historical programmes that may or may not complement each other.

In Chapter 10 we discuss how to set about deciding on a structure to deliver the biggest possible increase from the resources allocated to the programme. It will be a question of looking at objectives, thinking about the rules, and assessing which participants are likely to do what and by how much. You have the tools to do the job, but how do you put together a programme that is likely to produce higher performance rather than be ignored?

Structuring reward and recognition programmes

10

By now you will be aware of all the theory, examples of best practice and the basic tools of reward and recognition to be able to design your programme to be as effective as possible. But where do you start?

Many internal programme planners begin with the reward or incentive and then work backwards. It may be that the main internal sponsor has been persuaded by various marketing agencies that a particular destination or gift card or item of merchandise has been unusually popular in recent months and so deserves some consideration as the main reward. Or perhaps in previous years a particular reward mechanism was already in place. The 'brief' then comes to the organizer to make it happen. Unfortunately this approach is unlikely to be successful because it is the wrong way round.

All effective performance improvement programmes (PIPs) start with the four-stage process we have already been through: research, skills assessment, communication and reward. So before rushing off to book the venue for that specific incentive travel group or starting to renegotiate the bulk purchase of gift cards we need to review the research element, part of which is the key question: what do we hope to achieve?

In 1999 Dr Timothy McCarthy reviewed the multitude of theoretical papers about experiments in goal setting and wrote a short article for CEOs with regard to how to set goals for people in organizations. He made five key points:

- *Participation.* Joint goal setting between supervisors and their teams or individuals is much more effective than telling people what to do without discussion. Senior managers often mistake their leadership position as not having to ask for advice. There is perceived pressure on them simply to come up with the right technical answer almost without time for any thought process or time-consuming discussion. Team members tend to be much more loyal and responsive to discussion prior to decision making rather than solutions being dictated to them from on high. Such an approach makes for a more effective programme, because the participants have already made their technical amendments before the scheme is under way.

- *Specificity.* Goal setting can be effective only if the parameters for performance are absolutely clear. The pre-requirement is that the sponsor has discussed in detail what is required for the programme to be seen as successful for all the participants involved. For salespeople this means reasonable and attainable targets with various checks and balances in the rules to ensure that the competition is fair and attractive to those with the highest potential to improve. If there is to be a 'support' reward for those who help with the administration of the sales this needs to be thought through in terms of having clear measurements for achievement that are administration performance related.

- *Feedback.* Regular feedback is essential if you want a positive outcome. There should be measurement mechanisms in place to provide specific performance reports at all levels so that participants not only can see how they are doing against their peers but can learn how to modify their performance to do better. Many programmes fail because performance is published only at the end of the programme, by which time it is too late for participants to change their approach. The data must be available in a timely manner, as otherwise it cannot be used to reinforce behaviour while the campaign is progressing.

- *Challenging goals.* Without a programme, participants will deliver ordinary performance. To pay for the programme set-up and the rewards that go with higher-than-average achievement, the goals need to be stretching and challenging; otherwise you will simply be paying out for performance that you would have got anyway. There has to be an element of return on investment and going beyond what is normal; otherwise why would you bother to run it?

- *Commitment.* Participants must be personally committed to their goals, which must be relevant to their work situation. Many organizations run annual bonus schemes that promise to pay out often substantial sums if the organization achieves specific objectives, but if those objectives mean nothing to ordinary workers, such as stock price or market share, there will be little buy-in from participants unless they can see how their individual, local performance can affect the bigger picture.

So the very first task is to set some goals and objectives for the programme with a statement of what will be considered to be success by the end of the programme.

Setting sales goals

There is a substantial body of analytical work with regard to how to set sales targets and what the likelihood of better success may be by changing the parameters of what commission or bonuses to give to which type of seller for what type of contract sold. Much of it is from historical analysis of past sales and the state of the market, rising or falling. It may well be that there are new products involved or perhaps old products that need to be run out, dropped, or twinned with more recent products. This will change the nature of the emphasis on what product groups to sell. We should assume that this work has already been done and the cash-based element of the plan has been agreed.

The next task is then to see how the 'remuneration' plan can be supported by non-cash reward and recognition to heighten the effect of the sales remuneration scheme. The objectives of the non-cash programme will therefore complement the remuneration scheme and highlight the main thrust of sales activity. In most cases the non-cash programme echoes certain key elements of the cash plan as a kind of ongoing underlining of the sales strategy. Non-cash is easier to promote, because it usually entails specific desirable items or travel-related events, and the non-cash elements have a higher profile and tend to get talked about more than the cash elements.

What type of objectives could be considered in a typical non-monetary sales scheme? In Table 10.1 you can see that sales team objectives can be general or specific.

It is clear from Table 10.1 that some objectives are very close to what the cash reward scheme is designed to do. This is perfectly acceptable in that often mathematical-type sales plans work well for some people. But others never get to grips with the numbers and percentages that sales plans are full of and need to have the main objectives emphasized more graphically. More often there will be tactical or marginal activity that needs to be stressed at particular times of the year to take advantage of seasonal sales demand. Many sales managers believe that activity itself leads to more sales. Some programmes emphasize making more contacts or undertaking some promotional tasks that are linked to certain types of sale, as this will inevitably lead to more sales down the line.

Whatever objectives are chosen it is important not to choose measurable tasks that are at odds with the thrust of the main remuneration plan. For example, if the remuneration plan is largely to reward sales of the new products there is little point in having a non-monetary programme that rewards existing products, as salespeople will be receiving mixed messages about what to concentrate on. You should also take care to align programmes of related products and services. In complex sales scenarios such as automotive sales the same salesperson may be responsible for new unit sales, previously owned vehicles, finance and accessories all during the same day. Some element of orderly promotional marketing is needed to ensure that participants do not get confused about what their strategic tasks are.

TABLE 10.1 Typical sales team objectives

Increase sales in total.
Increase sales of specific products.
Increase sales to particular clients.
Increase sales through particular distributors.
Increases sales in specific local regions.
Increase sales of additional services.
Introduce new products and services.
Improve client retention.
Improve repeat orders from the same clients.
Improve the quality of sales (average revenue).
Sell off old stock; discount sales.
Respond to competitor activity.
Increase market share.
Improve outbound call rates and prospecting.
Improve administration and accuracy of paperwork.
Improve salesforce retention.
Improve team morale.
Recruit new salespeople.
Test product knowledge.

In large organizations there will be promotional and marketing activity for each of these technical sales areas, and it may be that they will not be as well coordinated with each other as they should be, as each division will have its own objectives to achieve during the financial year. 'Goal salience' is important to effective motivation planning. This means that those who are planning the promotions need to know what other, complementary product groups and services are doing so that the same salesperson is clear what he or she is expected to do over a given period. It could be argued that professional marketers should be able to do more than one thing at the same time, and they often do, depending on the strength of personality of the manager who supervises them. But, generally speaking, promotion should be simple and unambiguous, as by trying to achieve too much the result is that none of the programmes are as effective as they should be.

Following on from the principle of goal salience it would be perfectly practical to combine a new products incentive with an incentive for higher prospecting activity, as they both share the same objective of more sales of the same or similar products. The discussion would then hinge on what proportion of the reward should apply to which objective so that participants cannot earn more through prospecting activity than they can from actually closing sales. As praiseworthy as it is to be active, the organization needs to close product sales in volume at the right price to be successful in the final analysis of corporate results. Lots of misdirected activity and no sales make for poor performance.

Be careful what you wish for in terms of sales promotions to salesforces, as the more effectively they are promoted the more likely the promoted objectives will be met. An overriding emphasis on a particular scheme with highly attractive discretionary rewards could lead to unethical selling by some individuals. Typical behaviour could be selling to friends and relatives but then having the sales cancelled at some future date, claiming sales that have not been approved formally by the customer or buyer, offering bigger discounts than were authorized, double-counting sales, offering additional services that were not part of the costed package, under-the-table gifts to influence the sale decision, excessive corporate hospitality and many other informal practices to get the sale. There should be a finely crafted scorecard of checks and balances built into the programme rules to outlaw these and other activities, with some discretion at the end of the campaign to be able to verify that all sales claimed and allocated to certain individuals and teams are in fact bona fide. It is wise to plan for a period of settling or confirmation, possibly weeks, sometimes a few months in some corporate situations, so that the right individuals and teams win the rewards fairly. If not, you risk undermining your PIP strategy for future periods if participants feel that dubious practices are being sanctioned at the highest level by managers turning a blind eye to unfair activity, which does not benefit the organization in the long run.

Setting non-sales goals

Goal setting for non-sales parts of the organization is more difficult, as at first glance there is no obviously measurable output. For non-sales support staff the measurements require a leap of faith and will be drafted in the belief that achievement of certain levels of activity means a good job is being done. We have seen in Chapter 9 that by aligning say ideas schemes with the values of the organization you can reward compliant behaviour in the form of the number of value-aligned ideas that a particular person produces over a given period. The same principle applies in other types of activity. In Table 10.2 you can see how many administration activities are already measured and have a number value so that supervisors can check on average productivity. It is easy to see how these activities could form the basis of a non-monetary reward programme.

As with sales programmes any objectives need to be 'goal-salient' and not simply added because a sponsoring manager would like something done more efficiently. For example, one manager may want more recruits to come from employee suggestions rather than pay an external agency to produce candidates. Another may feel that it is vitally important to improve the effectiveness of dealing with inbound customer calls. Both are worthy but not necessarily related to each other. Some cooperation will be required to agree a series of complementary objectives that sit well together at certain periods of the year and so could be promoted together. Others may be best separated so that participants are clear what is required of them.

TABLE 10.2 Typical non-sales objectives

Reduce absenteeism.
Reduce costs.
Invite ideas for higher efficiency.
Promote teamwork and loyalty.
Promote inter-office cooperation.
Improve safety.
Improve timekeeping.
Increase productivity.
Improve employee retention.
Improve telephone skills.
Raise morale.
Monitor training effectiveness.
Improve budgetary control.
Increase sales referrals.
Recruit new colleagues.
Increase direct sales, if applicable.

All employees have key performance indicators (KPIs) in their everyday jobs, and each level of employee will have different KPIs. Non-monetary programme objectives are often based on these KPIs so that performance and incentives can be aligned. But KPIs for ordinary workers differ markedly from those of supervisors and higher-level managers. It makes sense therefore that the measures should change depending on the job role of the individual. However, they can still be part of the same non-cash programme, provided the activities being promoted are all clustered around the same general objective.

For example, an insurance organization may wish to improve the accuracy of its internal documentation. The fewer corrections there are in the process, the more quickly claims could be processed. Accuracy of form filling could be monitored by an independent audit team down to an individual level. Supervisors could then be measured by the average number of correctly completed forms from their team. Senior managers could be measured on the number of supervisors who complete a minimum level of accurate forms. The overall programme theme could be called 'Right First Time', but the various levels of participant will be measured under different criteria. The value of everyone being part of the same scheme is that all levels interact with each other to achieve common goals rather than some elements disengaging because they are not part of the reward scheme.

Using research to structure the programme

We have discussed research in Chapter 5. One of the great benefits of research is that in many instances it defines the structure for the planner without much dissension when it comes to getting internal agreement. If the participants are saying a particular thing is a 'must-have' in any forthcoming reward programme then there needs to be a compelling reason not to include it.

I conducted a human audit some years ago of a large retail bank salesforce of some 1,500 employed salespeople. The main complaint from the C-suite was that a substantial sum of money was being given to the same 100 salespeople, year after year, and there were doubts that the programme was effective in encouraging the more recently established salespeople to work harder and achieve higher levels of sales productivity. The human audit uncovered a number of technical changes that could be made. Most participants complained that there was only one big travel event per year based on volume of sales and that less experienced salespeople could not hope to qualify for it under the current rules. Others said that they only sold superannuation policies, so the programme did not cater for them in terms of being a competition. Still more said the current system was skewed towards those who worked in the big conurbations, as they had many more sales opportunities than rurally based employees.

The research told us how to structure the programme to appeal to more potential participants:

- Base qualification on improvement over the previous year, not pure volume sales.

- Introduce new categories of winners such as 'newcomers with less than two years' experience', specific product sales and regional leagues of qualifiers.

- Provide three incentive travel destinations of varying travel time and invent a gold, silver and bronze concept of qualification.

Clearly these changes would have a major effect on who might qualify, and there was much horse-trading with retail managers about whether they should be taking rewards away from established salespeople and giving them to younger recruits. The results were textbook in terms of performance improvement. Average productivity within the top quartile improved from 18,190 credits to 28,109 credits. It is true that some of the old-stagers complained bitterly that they could no longer qualify for the 'big travel event' because they could not achieve the level of conquest business that the younger people were producing, but this was the main reason the changes to the programme needed to be done.

It was clear from the research that changes were long overdue and that they were specific and relevant to the current organization, which was questioning the effectiveness of the considerable reward programme for its established salespeople. The improvement in top-quartile productivity was proof that, if researched effectively, great changes are possible. As in most marketing activity, if the 'customers' tell us what they want we would be foolish to ignore it, provided we can afford to meet their expectations.

Using skills in the structure

Skills development tends to be an unequal partner when structuring PIPs around the four categories of activity. In many instances no training is required, because this element is often handled outside the remit of PIP planning and in the majority of cases employees do have the skills to undertake the core tasks of their job. A PIP merely reminds them of what they should be doing and focuses attention on the key aims of the organization for specific periods.

But there are process improvements, which may be new skills or perhaps old skills that need to be relearned as they have now become even more vital to the overall success of the organization. In 2013 a major global digital imaging inventor and distributor decided to support a new incentive programme to its independent photographic and screen distributors by adding a skills element to its existing volume-driven reward programme. An online portal was developed known as a 'Zone'. Within this portal were technical details of all the new products and a series of technical quizzes that were communicated at regular intervals during a specific period. Participants were encouraged to take the quiz and submit their answers online. These answers were then factored into the overall incentive for products sold, resulting in a rank-order listing of distributor performance. In terms of rewards the participants could qualify for a new car, electronic products supplied by the sponsoring manufacturer and a series of gift card options for ongoing promotional activity. The key element of difference was the quiz, a skills development device, which underpinned the need to educate the ever-changing market in new products in a way that was integrated into the main incentive offering.

Skills do not always have to involve formal training and development. In many non-sales programmes, at some stage, there may be an element of presentation to a senior team to show the employees' case to be worthy of 'team of the month' or explain what their process idea was, as part of a wider recognition scheme. Many employees will not be accustomed to presenting their ideas in person and as a result may shy away from full participation in the programme, as they will be aware that the major awards can go only to those who are able to present their case in an effective manner. To encourage non-sales participants to take an active part in the recognition programme you may need to coach them in 'proposal presentation' so that they feel that they can be perceived as being professional to a senior team of adjudicators.

In many programmes there is often a qualification level that enables participants to be eligible for the scheme. In some distributor schemes manufacturers will allow only those who have attended their formal training courses to be enrolled in a reward scheme. This makes sense, as there is little point in rewarding independent workers who may be transient or not have the skills to talk about their products in a meaningful way. The role for the skills team is to identify which of their independent salespeople should be developed and therefore be enrolled at a later date into the rewards programme. By establishing a skills link with individuals, the manufacturer then has an open channel to promote other products to people it knows have the presentational skills to do it justice. It is a symbiotic relationship, even though there is no direct employment link.

In summary, skills provide the formal or informal link back to the individuals who are most likely to succeed in the programme and so make the system more efficient, with a better ROI.

Communication elements within the structure

Any programme structure is only as good as the data allow. Although non-sales schemes tend to run for at least 12 months, sales schemes can be as little as two weeks but more usually a quarter. The short duration poses particular issues to do with performance feedback. Programmes need to be built around the reporting patterns of the organization, as there will be no appetite to invent reporting measures just for the programme. Creating new reports is almost impossible if you are using a busy internal IT department with many other priorities, so the structure needs to take into account what reports will be used to keep participants up to date with how they are doing and how long it will take at the end to declare the undisputed winners. If the plan within the structure is to measure sales and quality you need to be sure that the two elements of data can be easily extracted from existing systems at the same time so that the reporting can be provided in a timely manner.

Communication at the end of the programme needs to be timely and accurate. In theory the best way to change behaviour is to reward as close to the change as possible. With online gift cards and distribution of goods being very efficient this should not be an issue. But communicating to all the participants about the winners is not as simple as it sounds. The bigger the end reward the more likely the sponsor will want to verify that the performance was achieved in a fair and reasonable manner. This suggests that within the structure notice of the announcement of winners needs to take into account the length of time it takes to do this. If the big reward is a group travel event it cannot be set up to take place within a few weeks of the end of the programme, as defining who has won will take several weeks. In addition to the announcement delay most people need to make private arrangements for children and dependants if they are going to be away, even for a few days. Practically speaking, an event should not be booked until at least eight weeks after the campaign has ended, and in some organizations it can be lengthier than this.

For those business sectors where retaining key staff may be an issue, such as insurance, real estate and recruitment, it may be wise to consider whether to delay the big travel events for several months after the end of the programme in order to encourage key participants to stay. You will often hear that ambitious salespeople will delay moving employers if they are wavering until they have attended the incentive event they have qualified for from the previous period. Some sales organizations deliberately delay the running of the major incentive event until the participants are at least halfway through the next programme to discourage them from leaving the organization. As a retention strategy it would be better if they were to investigate issues more professionally and confront the problem head on if it is systemic, but delaying rewards could be just one of many factors that help to retain key people.

Reward elements within the structure

We have dealt with reward choices in Chapter 8, but when it comes to structure you need to choose an appropriate hierarchy to suit the participant database. There are no set principles, but it is very likely that you want to have a tiered structure of rewards, because not all participant contributions are the same.

Typically, hosted incentive travel will come at the top end in terms of cost per head with fewer participants at a fixed package price, and gift cards at the bottom with very low denominations. In this way you are able to reward the highest number of winning participants at the lowest cost. If you have a regional structure you may wish to reward leading participants locally with an event, but this should clearly not upstage the big national event. In the same way it is perfectly possible to provide gift cards in large denominations for the most important performers. But at every level the perceived value of the rewards should reflect the structure in a reinforcing way. It would be inequitable to be offering a highly perceived reward in a low-achievement category, as other participants would complain that the effort did not match the reward. Devising the rewards distribution to fit the structure may not be easy, as there will be conflicting views about what works and what does not as an appropriate reward choice. You may need to consider several iterations in terms of value and actual items before you settle on an appropriate tiered structure that appears to the participants to be fair and provide sufficient reward for the perceived effort.

Constructing the rules

Over many years programme planners have invented ever more complex rules and scheme structures to deal with the various anomalies that crop up when planning what participants have to do to win the rewards. They mostly apply to sales programmes, but in some circumstances they could also apply to non-sales schemes.

Problem 1: unequal chances to win

In populated parts of the world there is more opportunity to find new clients than in sparsely populated areas. This is a fact of sales geography. But in the quest to ensure that participants perceive their chances of winning as fair PIP planners have incorporated 'leaguing' into their rules so that all participants feel they have as good a chance as anyone else in the scheme of qualifying. This technique is also the antidote to those who like to run programmes based on absolute volume.

As in the banking example mentioned earlier in the chapter, simply providing rewards for those who are well established anyway is not an incentive. It could be argued that you are wasting resources by rewarding those who need to make the least effort. If all participants were ranked in order of sales volume there would be few surprises at the end of the programme in terms of winners, and those who were less established would feel that organizationally inspired schemes did not work for them until they had accumulated a greater volume of existing clients and contacts.

Equal leagues

Within a sales environment leaguing involves placing participants within a peer group so that similar individuals or businesses compete on a like-for-like basis and the top-ranked qualifiers from each league qualify for the major rewards.

Example: 99 distributors producing between 5 million and 100 million credits in terms of supplier sales turnover. Nine incentive travel rewards available for the highest-performing distributors.

Solution: Create three equal leagues based on current turnover with awards for the top three in each league. (Three winners × three leagues = nine winners.) Nine winners will then be produced with a 1 in 11 chance of winning rather than an open competition where unless you are a high-volume distributor you are highly unlikely to qualify. (See Table 10.3.)

TABLE 10.3 Equal leagues

League 1	League 2	League 3
Dealer 1	Dealer 34	Dealer 67
Dealer 2	Dealer 35	Dealer 68
. . .	. . .	. . .
Dealer 33	Dealer 66	Dealer 99
1 in 11 chance	1 in 11 chance	1 in 11 chance

If the leagues are split based on turnover from say 5 million to 20 million, over 20 million to 49 million, and over 49 million to 100 million or more, it can be seen how similar-size organizations will be competing with their peers. One perceived downside is that sponsors may feel that they are rewarding lower-turnover distributors with a reward that should really be going to their biggest distributors. This can be remedied by introducing the concept of unequal leagues.

Unequal leagues

In this new scenario the three leagues could be split unevenly based on volume so that inclusion in league 1 requires 50 million sales or more, inclusion in league 2 requires 20 million to 49 million, and inclusion in league 3 requires less than 20 million. The effect will be to increase the chances that the higher-turnover distributors will win the major travel reward. In league 1 there will be a 1 in 2 chance of winning, league 2 participants will have a 1 in 6.33 chance, and in league 3 the chances will be 1 in 24.3. (See Table 10.4.)

In Table 10.4 you can see that with just six distributors in league 1 the biggest distributors have a 1 in 2 chance to achieve the major incentive travel award. By mathematical necessity the other leagues' chances of winning have reduced, but the perception is still that this is a fairer system than simply rewarding the biggest-volume distributors as in the old system. The leaguing system could apply to

TABLE 10.4 Unequal leagues

League 1	League 2	League 3
Dealer 1	Dealer 7	Dealer 26
Dealer 2	Dealer 8	Dealer 27
. . .	. . .	. . .
Dealer 6	Dealer 25	Dealer 99
1 in 2 chance	1 in 6.3 chance	1 in 24.3 chance

geography, type of product, length of service, level of funding, level of competence or indeed any other relevant measure that attempts to minimize the perception that individuals cannot compete at the highest level for the major rewards. In essence it is a handicap system that attempts to level the playing field.

The leaguing principle can be applied to categories of non-sales employees too. It may be that employees could be put in leagues by division, length of service, level of training or some other defining characteristic so that they compete only with their peer group and not with everyone in the organization.

Problem 2: fixed winners or reach the target?

One of the most common issues when constructing a reward scheme is to devise the rules in such a way that there is either a fixed number of winners or an open-ended structure. Having a fixed number of winners is attractive to sponsors, because they can see a fixed level of expenditure for their initial investment, but this is less effective as a motivator for the participants, as they will often perceive who the winners are most likely to be and so not compete in a positive way. It is common for sales incentives to fail because the participants in a fixed winners system have already factored in who is most likely to win the major rewards.

In motivational terms it is much more effective for participants to aim for a specific objective or personal target and win a reward if they achieve the goal, regardless of who else has achieved the same target in the organization or within the distribution chain.

> Example: 100 salespeople compete for a major travel incentive over 12 months but only the top 10 can qualify, based on rank-order volume of sales, because the travel budget per head is a fixed amount. You could, of course, league them, but having done that you still have the issue of having to beat others to gain one of the top spots in the various leagued categories.

> Solution: Analyse last year's sales performance and establish a volume target that is challenging and reward those who achieve a high level of sales volume within each qualifying category, regardless of how many there may be.

The result will be individuals attempting to achieve a specific sales goal regardless of whoever else has achieved it. They will be competing with themselves rather than others. This structure is sometimes known as 'Beat your best'. Sponsors may argue that the number of winners could be many more than they had allowed for in the budget, but this raises the question about incremental profit for each sale above target. We deal with this in Chapter 11. As long as the target represents an incremental gain for the organization the additional travel places should pay for themselves.

Problem 3: aiming for personal targets

A further sophistication of the individual targets system is the 'commit to win' or 'bid 'n' make' format. In this scenario participants declare at the outset what they are aiming for against a pre-published list of rewards.

> Example: John Doe decides he can achieve 5 million credits in the sales period and commits to it. In the published list of rewards this equates to a family holiday in Barbados.

Solution: The sponsor researches and promotes a list of rewards, rising in value, that are pegged to specific volumes of sales. Individual participants aim for those rewards during the period. If they overachieve they receive the rewards plus additional enhancements. If they underachieve they get the choice of the lower-level rewards below their target list.

Such a system can be very effective, as it personalizes the rewards to individuals and they have something specific to aim for that is not simply a number. When you have specific items this also provides plenty of scope for promotion both generally and specifically, which creates further discussion and debate between participants.

A further variant could be to allow participants to 'bid' for each other's rewards by using accumulated credits as bidding chips. In this system there is only one reward at each level of credits. The more chips you have the higher the reward level you can bid for, so it would be possible for you to 'steal' another person's reward by out-bidding them for it. Or the chips could be split and used for several lower-level rewards instead of one big reward. This system relies on a fair amount of good will between participants who view incentive competitions as an opportunity to measure themselves against their peers rather than to obtain a one-off reward with no reference to anyone else. It also requires some software that can deal with the bidding process in a straightforward way.

Problem 4: setting more challenging targets

Most achievement targets are linear: do this–get that. If you achieve twice as much, you might expect to receive twice the reward. However, this is not an especially motivational structure, as it is relatively easy to relate effort to reward and many participants baulk at simply repeating the effort all over again when they have already been working very hard to achieve the first level.

Example: Jane Smith is a top achiever and regularly qualifies for whatever reward is put up by the organization as an incentive. When she reaches the highest level, such as qualifying for the

TABLE 10.5 Escalator example

Level	Payment
Base target	1,000
110 per cent	2,000
120 per cent	4,000
130 per cent	10,000

overseas travel event, she makes less effort and waits for the next incentive to come along.

Solution: The sponsor could introduce an escalator that offers additional rewards or enhancements for non-linear achievement above target. (See Table 10.5.)

In the escalator system, rewards above target are then stepped up in unequal stages with more lavish rewards, leaving the attainment targets equal. The value of the rewards is considerably more than could be earned in the standard programme, but these calculations are based on the chances of reaching such elevated levels being highly unlikely. For example, at the top level you might offer a new car in the full knowledge that it is unlikely that anyone will reach this level based on historical performance. This would be highly promotable as a headline reward, but those who are high achievers will realize that performance to pay for it would have to be historically very high. The escalator therefore deals with stretching those at the higher levels who may achieve easily the target at an early stage in the general incentive period and feel there is no further reason for them to keep achieving as they have already hit the highest level possible.

Problem 5: modest budget, large number of participants

A common issue within large organizations is large numbers of participants but a relatively small average per-head rewards budget. Many non-sales programme budgets cannot simply be increased, as the ROI from non-sales employees raising their performance is rarely simple to prove and most senior managers would err on the side of caution.

> Example: A major call-handling firm employs over 30,000 people on a part-time basis to handle incoming calls from a variety of big brand-name clients. It would like to introduce an effective incentive programme to reward exceptional employees for delivering the organization's core values, but it has only 100,000 credits.

> Solution: The only way to solve this budget shortfall is to introduce a sweepstake or lottery system whereby graduations in achievement earn tickets in a sweepstake, with the principle being that the more tickets you have the more likely you will win something substantial.

This way of dealing with a modest budget per head works well for those who may not be experienced in being participants in an incentive scheme. The unknown element of possibly winning a big reward by chance clearly has its merits. But it is important to sense-check what effort participants are being asked to make in return for just the chance to win something.

A better structure may be to allocate some rewards to the 'top team' so there is something specific to aim for as well as a lottery element for general activity. If the entire scheme is based on chance it is highly likely that a participant who engages very little with the programme could win the largest reward and so undermine the entire initiative. Perhaps a better way to deal with such potential downsides is to allow only those who have qualified for say 10 sweepstake tickets, according to the rules, to be in the draw for the major rewards. It is not an ideal solution, but it is preferable to introducing nothing simply because you have been defeated by the mathematics of large numbers and small resources.

Problem 6: all or nothing

Professional and technical organizations often struggle with rewards for non-sales staff. Where it is difficult to allocate credits for specific sales, as many rely on financial documentation or technical support staff, they tend to offer group incentives for everyone.

> Example: A software corporate with 300 employees wants to reward its entire team if they can achieve 120 per cent of their sales budget. The plan is to take everyone in the organization on a travel trip, even the cleaners.
>
> Solution: Targets can be promoted that offer a tiered level of rewards for all, depending on overall corporate performance. The ultimate would be for everyone to travel overseas as a result, but if you fall short the tiered system allows you to fund a home-country reward and lower still a series of gift cards. In this way, whatever the outcome, everyone gets something.

The issue with all-or-nothing schemes is that if the organization falls short of its headline target then no one is rewarded. This can be highly demotivational for those who excel or who have made special efforts during the year. If the plan is for everyone to benefit in a simple way then it would be better to run a tiered programme say from 80 per cent achievement through to 120 per cent achievement with three threshold levels of reward such as three potential event destinations so that the team has something to work towards. It is also likely that end-of-year financial results can be manipulated at the highest level to show a certain level of performance if you have ongoing sales projects or licensed work. In such cases, declaring a definitive number for the year end may be problematical if the numbers are running very close to the pay-out level. It would be advisable to run the programme based on revenue rather than profits, as it may be difficult to persuade people to waive their reward simply to boost profits for the business owners in any given year.

Problem 7: lack of uptake

Manufacturers often compete with their competitors to get a share of their market through various outlets that they do not own. It is hard to get cooperation from independent distributors when so many other suppliers are trying to influence the same retail chain of salespeople.

FIGURE 10.1 Effect of fast-start on revenues

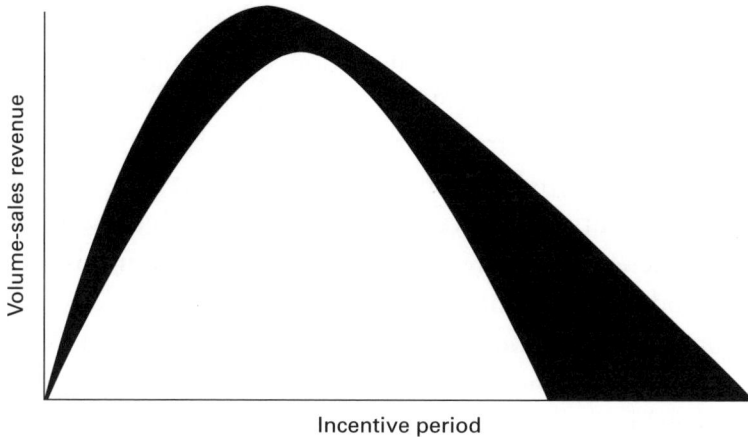

Incentive period

(y-axis: Volume-sales revenue)

Solution: One way to get early share of mind is to build into the structure a 'fast-start' element. In essence you offer double the credits for performance achieved during the first month or the first half of the programme period.

This has the effect of your business partners giving your scheme more support than would otherwise be the case. Volumes are pulled forward earlier than you might have expected over any given period, and because the partner gets into the habit of recommending your products there will be a natural tail-off that will last longer than the actual closing date of the programme.

In Figure 10.1 you can see that if you were simply to run the programme without the fast-start element the distribution of revenue would follow the normal bell curve. If you introduce a fast-start element it has the effect of pulling sales forward as well as creating a longer tail of residual sales after the campaign has ended. In effect the benefit in additional revenue is represented by the area in black.

Programme length

There is no definitive length for a programme to run. In many non-sales situations it could run indefinitely over many years, but there seems to be a natural tendency to tie it into the financial year so that any funding can be related back to improvements in performance. That said, it is usual for organizations to research and review their non-sales, values-driven schemes every three years or so on the basis that the world changes rapidly, as do the communication media, and that a rigorous examination of any scheme's effectiveness should be undertaken in the same way that business strategy is reviewed on a regular basis.

Within the sales environment, programmes that are strategic tend to run for 12 months or more. But as most tasks within a sales scheme tend to be tactical in nature requiring short-term emphasis on a few specific products or points of promotion it is more likely that the programme will run from one week to three months. It may be that there is an annual programme to reward and recognize regular and persistent achievement but with tactical spikes of a shorter nature to underpin some promotional activity. Some communicators find it useful to establish an annual theme, with additional themes for the shorter, tactical promotions. The perception from the participants is that there is a long-term, values-based aim such as 'Excel', but part of it should be a shorter need for specific activities such as 'Beat your best', which adds to the overall strategic goal.

Structures change with the market

The purpose of the structure is to best reflect the profile of the participants and how to encourage them to take part and support the programme. If that means adapting the rewards to appeal to larger numbers of the audience, setting up leagues, introducing a fast-start element or completely revamping the scheme to be more in keeping with the economic situation from time to time, then the programme will work. As in all areas of organizational excellence, standing still is rarely the best option.

There is no doubt that everyone could be well rewarded for incremental effort if there were no budget constraints, but the allocation of scarce resources is what most organizations grapple with. In Chapter 11 we examine how best to use a finite budget and what to expect in terms of costs when it comes to running PIPs. You may be surprised to discover that the reward element is only half the story, quite literally.

Setting the budget

11

Setting a suitable budget for reward and recognition programmes is both an art and a science. It has to have enough resource to appeal to the entire workforce and reward them accordingly, but equally you should not be paying for performance that is already contracted. By virtue of the fact that large numbers of people are involved, the budget itself will not be insignificant. But what are the parameters and how easy is it to determine what the final cost will be, if we are dealing with the unknowable performance improvement of many individuals as they work independently on their day-to-day tasks?

Defining the budget for a performance improvement programme (PIP) is no different from setting a budget for any other kind of important expenditure. The largest element of cost is likely to be the reward element, so certain assumptions need to be made about what degree of reward may be appropriate. There will be some fixed costs. The eventual total spend will depend on how well the scheme is used and supported by the employees or the distributors. Some flexibility is required by the sponsors in terms of overachievement, but if the programme does overachieve that should be good news for everyone.

Many organizations investigate up front whether the programme can be self-funding in the sense that the initiative pays for itself over time. Establishing a breakeven measure of success for the scheme from the outset not only is good business practice but will reassure any doubters who may feel that it is a 'nice-to-have' scheme, but only if it can be afforded.

Incremental profit for sales incentives

The ideal financial objective of any PIP is to establish the point at which it becomes self-funding and therefore is winning the argument that it is better to have such a programme than not have one. For sales incentives and reward programmes the budget turns on what increase in sales is expected. Here is an example of the principle of incremental profit and how to work out what sales target to set.

Self-funding example

Within a defined campaign period firm A is estimating it will achieve 1 million revenue. (It is not important which currency the revenue will be in for the purposes of the example so I have not shown any currency denomination.) A sales incentive scheme is proposed at a time of the year when sales are usually good, all things taken into account. The plan is therefore to extend the traditionally positive sales period by a few months or more, if possible. (In general sales incentives are run in good periods rather than bad periods, as the market factors for bad periods will probably not be solved by simply offering an incentive.) But how much can firm A afford to spend per million of revenue?

1 The sales director reckons that by offering sales-linked rewards he would be able to increase sales by 20 per cent. The revenue target would therefore be 1.2 million.

2 Firm A calculates that additional revenue earns contributing profits of 35 per cent. By applying this percentage to the additional or incremental revenue we arrive at an extra profit amount of 70,000.

3 In normal trading an allowance of 33.3 per cent is made to pay for generating new business under the headings of promotion. By applying this number to the extra profit generated we arrive at a promotional allowance of 23,310.

4 If we assume that the costs of launch and promotion are fixed we can assume that the actual budget available for rewards

will be 23,310 per 1 million of revenue. In other words the rewards amount is between 2 per cent and 3 per cent of normal trading revenue for the period.

Summary

- Expected revenue without incentive, 1 million.

- Expected revenue with incentive, 1.2 million.

- Incremental revenue, 200,000.

- Profit margin at 35 per cent, 70,000.

- Rewards budget at 33.3 per cent of additional profit, 23,310.

If we then compare the rewards budget to the level of additional sales, we establish a breakeven number of 11.7 per cent. (Express 23,310 as a percentage of 200,000.) The sales team has to produce 11.7 per cent more sales revenue than expected to cover the additional rewards cost. This suggests that the campaign target for making the incentive self-funding would be 1.12 million. Overachievement beyond that target would produce revenue at 35 per cent of sales, so it would be good to go beyond 1.12 million, as from then on the programme is self-funding.

This example sits well with the gut feel of most sales directors, who will tell you without any   analysis that, if you offer rewards for sales over and above bonuses or commissions, 10 per cent would be the minimum but with good promotion 20 per cent would be a reasonable success level to achieve. We have already seen in Chapter 3 that performance within sales schemes can vary between 10 per cent extra and 50 per cent extra depending on the economic situation and the standing of the firm when compared with its competitors. There is also the phenomenon that organizations that are new to PIPs tend to overachieve against the norm in the early years. More mature sectors and organizations that use sales incentives on a regular basis experience a certain amount of diminishing returns, as both the salespeople and the buyers get used to running incentives on a regular basis. The trick is to keep the promotion fresh and think constantly how to make the offer different and special, even though in the final analysis additional rewards are being offered for extra effort.

Every organization is different. It may be that promotion or the administration of such a programme is a significant cost and so should be included in the self-funding calculation. There is no one-size-fits-all solution, but in general the set-up and promotion are insignificant compared with the incremental profit, especially if the revenue generated is in the millions.

Incremental profit for employee programmes

We have already stated that measuring employee performance improvement to arrive at a breakeven point presents more challenges than revenue-generating programmes. Ideas schemes are relatively straightforward, as you can calculate the extra revenue or the cost savings resulting from the total of all the ideas and compare that figure with the cost of setting up the scheme and distributing rewards.

It is possible to set up a breakeven point beforehand by establishing the cost of setting up and managing the programme together with the rewards estimate and then simply waiting for the ideas to catch up. If we assume that a programme for 1,000 employees has been estimated at 100,000, including rewards, this sum will have been based on a certain number of ideas being generated during the programme. If you have no historical data to use you could do worse than begin with say one idea per engaged employee each quarter, which would generate 2,000 ideas in a year if engagement was 50 per cent. Of those 2,000 ideas, there will be say 20, so 1 per cent, that will produce the significant cost savings and revenue generation to cover the costs and more besides. So the metrics become:

- cost of set-up and rewards;
- engagement level;
- average number of ideas generated;
- total financial benefit from ideas.

Every employee base is different, and you may be able to get help from your national suggestion schemes association to estimate the

TABLE 11.1 Financial impact of engagement: will 'engagement talent' impact our financials?

Corporate "weighted average" total salary and benefit cost:	Performance delivered	Estimated organization employee base: 25,000 $ 89,750	CURRENT financial impact of employee engagement	
Engagement level		Bottom line impact	% Organization	Financial impact
LEVEL 4 Fully engaged	125%	Organization GAINS $22,438 per year	10%	$ 56,093,750
LEVEL 3 Engaged	100%	Employee delivers an organization 'value' equal to the costs (salary + benefit)	65%	$ –
LEVEL 2 Somewhat engage	75%	Organization LOSES $(22,438) per year	20%	$ (112,187,500)
LEVEL 1 Disengagement	50%	Organization LOSES $(44,875) per year	5%	$ (56,093,750)
			Annual impact of engagement	$ (112,187,500)
		What is the financial impact per share? 997,839,000 shares		(0.11)

likely number of suggestions per employee in your sector so that you can build your business case. As for engagement levels there is a formula devised by Allan Schweyer (2009) of the Human Capital Institute that sets out the approach to measuring the impact of engagement on share values. (See Table 11.1.)

In the example in Table 11.1 you can see that high levels of disengagement caused a financial drag on the organization of some $112 million. By raising the number of those 'fully engaged' to 20 per cent the positive impact would be $56 million. Clearly this is a large enterprise of 25,000 employees, and as a result the gains will be large as well. But in the context of over $50 million extra revenue the intervention cost in set-up and rewards is likely to be less than $5 million. This would represent a very small cost for such huge gains.

The assumption is that the organization already has an unequivocal way to measure engagement and that other interventions are happening to raise engagement levels, not just a single programme, yet to be introduced. For these reasons it is impossible to provide a catch-all plan to 'prove' that employee programmes can be costed beforehand to deliver a guaranteed profit. There is a certain element of belief involved that by including employees in the performance improvement process then profits will come. The organizational evidence is still anecdotal but, with more and more studies being published and initiatives such as the Enterprise Engagement Alliance-inspired Good Company Stock Index (GCSI) in the United States, the concept of higher engagement = higher profits is growing stronger each month within business circles.

Budget headings

Whether you are able to calculate an ROI or not, there is still work to be done on costing out the programme and deciding if the outlay is worth the risk. All recognition and reward programmes have an element of fixed cost and variable cost. The fixed cost includes the set-up and management of the scheme. The variable costs are linked to what rewards are distributed, as no one knows until the programme is under way how actively the participants will engage with the scheme. Variable costs may also include the number of participants in your programme.

Fixed costs

Here is a list of potential fixed costs in menu style. Not all programmes require every category of cost. If your organization is large enough you may well be able to supply these services in-house, which would make breakeven and your risk less challenging:

- research and consultancy on programme structure;
- licence or fee for platform development;
- creative branding, image rights;
- copywriting;
- video, YouTube or similar scripting;
- printed materials, collation, packaging;
- launch venue hire, briefings, cascade costs, production;
- skills manuals or modules;
- external or internal management of the programme;
- reward event, if a hosted group;
- post-event research.

The list could be much longer depending on the complexity of your programme. The important point is to list all the costs that will not change, regardless of participant involvement. In effect this list represents your risk outlay. If, for whatever reason, no one participates, this sum represents the costs that you cannot recover. The only reduction may be the fee charges from any external agency, which would not charge their monthly administration fee if the programme did not go ahead or required no assistance after launch.

Variable costs based on participants

Some of the above costs may be variable depending on the number of participants involved. In general they may not be significant once the set-up has been paid for, but it is worth remembering that a programme for 1,500 participants may be no more expensive to create than one for 100 so consider involving as many groups as possible to get the maximum return on the initial set-up:

- ongoing administration of participant activity and redemptions;
- copies of printed literature;
- distribution of materials;
- rewards;
- reward-based handling fees;
- ongoing consultancy;
- mid-campaign research and online surveys.

Some agencies offer a 'win fee' whereby a fee is paid out only if the programme meets certain criteria of success. Although this sounds attractive when considering which external supplier, if any, to appoint at the outset, it may be difficult to establish after the programme has finished who was at fault if the scheme fails to deliver the expected performance levels. It is probably wiser to choose a business partner on the basis of track record and reliability to get things done professionally rather than saving perceived costs on a win-fee basis.

Setting an appropriate reward level

It is likely that the reward element of the budget will be the largest single category of spend within the PIP budget. The more participants there are the larger the rewards become as a proportion of the overall budget or expenditure for the programme, unless you have already set a fixed number of rewards. But what is an appropriate level of reward?

Sales rewards

There is no fixed formula that you can use to establish the reward budget. It is likely that most salespeople will also receive a contingency payment based on sales in addition to a salary. This suggests that an incentive reward does not need to be as big as the sales commission but large enough to encourage extra effort.

A rule of thumb from experience is to allocate pro rata around 0.5 to 1 per cent of the salary bill to provide the rewards for an incentive programme. For example, someone earning 40,000 competing for a three-month period would normally earn 10,000. A non-cash reward of 1,000 for overachieving during the period and being declared one of the top 5 per cent of achievers would be reasonable. This is enough to fund a lavish travel event in most markets. Those who achieve at lower levels could receive anywhere from 100 to 250, say.

Employee rewards

Employee rewards tend to be more token than lavish on the basis that their jobs are not at risk if they underperform. Most leaders agree that rewards for employee programmes should recognize that above-average effort has been made but that they should not become cash substitutes. If participants become dependent on the reward programme to pay their bills at the end of the month there is clearly something wrong with the standard remuneration package. A general rule of thumb is a quarter of 1 per cent of salary. For example, an administrator who earns 20,000 in a financial year might expect to earn 50 for above-average achievement. In this way the focus of the programme is on the tasks involved and the engagement levels of employee groups rather than the reward itself.

These percentages are merely suggestions and can vary greatly depending on what employees already receive in various benefits and salary and their attitude to contingency rewards. In some professional organizations where the work itself is the main driver of satisfaction a gift card may be perceived as irrelevant. Those who work in repetitive administrative roles may welcome the reward as an entertaining distraction that helps them focus on key tasks that they might otherwise just ignore.

Budgeting for variable rewards

This is where the art of budgeting should be applied. Not all levels of performance should be rewarded equally. As we have already discovered in Chapter 10, in any given scheme there will be a fixed number of event rewards that can be costed on a per-head basis. There will also be some variable rewards based on sales gained or ideas submitted that will require an estimate based on previous performance or a knowledge of industry statistics.

In such cases the reward element will be a range of costs rather than a definitive cost because the performance levels are unpredictable. The only way to define such a budget exactly is to offer a fixed number of rewards to those who rank to a certain level. This is not ideal, as it tends to reward those who would have done or be likely to do the task anyway. Some guesswork is required to estimate the likely reward levels, supported by the rules to ensure that the rewards do not overshadow the main thrust of the programme, which is to promote improved performance.

It is always useful to make some assumptions when creating a workable budget, as otherwise it is difficult to sketch out what the proportions are. Depending on your tax regime the proportions will change. But, to give an example, if the UK basic tax rate is 20 per cent, Table 11.2 shows a likely budget in terms of headings for an incentive. The tax allowance needs to be included at 25 per cent, as it will need to be grossed up for budgeting purposes.

From this example it is clear that taking taxes into account a budget of approximately 100,000 is likely to provide a rewards budget of only 55 per cent. This is a useful ratio to be aware of, as most sponsors will simply divide the budget by the number of participants and do their calculations of average reward from that base rather than considering the fixed costs and removing them first. It is possible to

TABLE 11.2 Budget summary based on approximately 100,000

1.	Set-up and launch	12,000
2.	Ongoing administration	18,000
3.	Rewards	55,000
4.	Tax grossed up at 25%	13,750
		98,750

raise the level of reward allocated by reducing the set-up costs and the ongoing fees, but this is a point for negotiation with the supplier.

Whatever rewards budget you settle on there will still be an amount to pay in tax, unless you decide that participants should pay the tax at their marginal rate. If all the qualifiers are higher-rate taxpayers, say 40 per cent, then the grossed-up rate will be 66 per cent of the reward element. For higher-rate taxpayers it is debatable whether they should be included if 66 per cent of their reward allocation needs to be earmarked for benefits tax.

Procurement and contracting

Most sponsors have a policy of procurement for major external purchases. Reward programmes can involve substantial sums, as the rewards usually relate to the number of people employed. If the programme administration and also the rewards are provided by external suppliers, this purchase is normally managed by professional buyers who work for the sponsor.

Dealing with and through procurement

In recent years both suppliers and procurers have come to terms with how best to cost and compare reward and recognition offerings. In the early days there was some resistance amongst suppliers to adapting their proposals to the needs of procurement departments on the basis that this service was a creative product that could not easily be compared. How much is a good idea worth? But in truth the majority of programme suppliers include a relatively fixed number of services, which can be compared, like for like, with the only differential being the creative theming. On that basis it would be up to the HR or marketing buyer to choose to pay a premium for an interesting idea rather than simply choosing the supplier with the least expensive administration fees.

More involvement from professional buyers has resulted in lower fees for large programmes and more scrutiny in terms of what is included in the fees and how the decisions to appoint a particular supplier are being made. Some sponsors use external agencies to manage the buying process, such as Accenture, and the purchase is treated like any other supply. This has its challenges for both parties, as often the buying agency does not fully understand the concept of outsourcing rewards and recognition expertise. Decisions based purely on cost can go awry. Experience of how recognition programmes work in practice may be more valuable to a sponsor than half of one percentage point off the cost of rewards, for example. But this is difficult to get across within the context of a global buying platform, which may not be designed to enable either buyer or supplier to ask the right questions.

One other consequence of the professionalism of the buying process is that most of the external suppliers to this market are not big enough in resources to be able to spend time completing lengthy and sometimes incomprehensible procurement platforms, designed for the purchase of large-scale industrial items rather than with creative services in mind. This leads to just three or four large suppliers in many markets competing on an ongoing basis for all the major projects, with very little to choose between them in terms of creative approach and new ideas.

One missing factor when the sponsor uses a buying platform is the ability to be able to talk directly to the supplier to assess whether the sponsor will be able to fashion a good working relationship with the supplier. Most programmes have a development and management cycle of at least 18 months, so it is important that the supplier is able to establish a good working relationship with its reward and recognition provider. Once the shortlist is drawn up, there is the opportunity to discuss matters face to face with the sponsor, but by that time the smaller, more creative suppliers have been rejected.

Terms and conditions

As with any other purchase for an organization there will be a contract to sign and some terms to agree to. Here is a list of standard terms that the buyer will need to be aware of when outsourcing programme administration:

- creative and administration fees;
- expenses;
- sponsor amendments;
- terms of payment;
- purchase tax, if applicable;
- service levels;
- cancellation or suspension;
- copyright;
- legality (of promotion);
- non-assignment;
- confidentiality;
- legal jurisdiction;
- dispute resolution;
- exchange rates, for overseas travel.

If you have experience of legal contracting then this list holds no surprises. But if you are used to agreeing to promotions or marketing services arranged by a simple exchange of e-mails, it is useful to understand what the implications of some of these so-called standard terms are to avoid issues later on if standards are not met or you wish to change suppliers.

Fees

Fees may be based on the amount of rewards administered, so they are contingent on the amount being claimed rather than the amount available in the budget. No sponsor should pay for administration that does not happen.

Expenses

Many suppliers do not charge for travel and subsistence in the management of the programme, as this is covered by a contingency in the hourly fees. But site inspections for any overseas events in connection with the reward or recognition programme will be at cost and need to be budgeted for. Some consultancies levy a charge of between 1 and 3 per cent of the fee or even the expenditure for 'administration, communication, faxes' and other administrative costs. This should be queried, as the cost of communication is minimal these days.

Sponsor amendments

Any changes to the design or text are often charged as extras, so be aware that there is a cost to failing to agree internally what the communication items should look like and say. This would also apply to changes in the software coding, so make changes only if they are absolutely necessary.

Terms of payment

This item is probably the most disputed contractual detail of the entire programme. Cash flow can be an important issue for suppliers, especially if the reward budget is a large amount and the supplier is duty bound by its service level agreements (SLAs) to deliver rewards to participants in a timely manner. The sponsor needs to keep its part of the bargain and provide the reward budgets on schedule so that the participants receive their rewards when they are expected.

Purchase tax

Most suppliers present costs without purchase tax calculations on the basis that most buyers can claim the purchase tax back. If you are unable to reclaim purchase tax this will represent a significant over-spend on the budget when the final bills are put forward for payment if you haven't factored for this in your budget.

Service levels

Service level agreements are commonplace in the supply of administrative schemes, but they should be carefully scrutinized for their practicality. Although gift cards can be distributed within 24 hours and many suppliers offer this service, there will be periods such as public holidays and weekends when this is not possible through the usual channels.

Cancellation or suspension

Cancellation terms are often worded in favour of the sponsor, but when running people programmes the effect on the participants of such drastic action as cancelling a supplier's services could be self-defeating. Whatever is happening in the background, they need to receive their rewards, so robust replacement plans need to be in place before breaking irrevocably with a supplier.

Copyright

The copyright for the administration system rests with the supplier unless you specifically contract to buy it. This could be quite expensive, as the same system is probably used, with a few amendments, to service your competitor's programmes, and no supplier would agree to remove its ability to be able to sell similar services to other sponsors. It is, however, normal for the supplier to grant copyright to you for the creative designs, as these are unlikely to be of use to anyone else but the sponsor.

Legality (of promotion)

In some jurisdictions some types of incentive may be illegal if they create undue or unfair pressure on individuals. If you are intending to roll out a reward or recognition programme internationally you should check that there are no legal restrictions in doing so.

Non-assignment

This refers to subcontracting key parts of the administration to a third party. It is common practice to use freelance specialists to create elements of reward programmes, from creative design through to software code writing. This can be very cost-effective for the sponsor, who may not want the overhead involved in buying all the services from one supplier. But the sponsor needs to be aware of who is delivering the core services, as there is nothing more irritating than trying to manage a people programme through a broker who may not be aware of all the nuances that such a project involves.

Confidentiality

This is a standard term in most supplier contracts, but in the case of reward and recognition programmes the key issue is data protection of the individual participants. The supplier needs to spell out how its information is protected and what restrictions there are on its later use as a promotional tool.

Legal jurisdiction

It is worth checking what the legal jurisdiction for disputes is. It would be difficult to sue the supplier for the non-delivery of services if the case had to be pursued through foreign courts.

Dispute resolution

Ask the supplier to explain the process for any disagreement about what was asked for and what was delivered, complete with an arbitration route if the disagreement cannot be resolved. PIPs can be very complex in terms of detail, so it is wise to establish how to resolve an impasse should it crop up at some future date.

Exchange rates

This term would only affect the cost of overseas travel if that is part of your reward package. It is standard practice to declare at what exchange rate the initial travel proposal was costed. Currency exchange rates can be volatile in certain parts of the world, and it is unlikely that a supplier will wish to be held accountable some 12 months later for a travel package price that has changed substantially since it was first costed.

Choosing an appropriate supplier

Reward and recognition suppliers come in all shapes and sizes, from individual consultants to multinational programme organizers. It makes sense to choose a supplier that best matches your needs, but you should be aware as a buyer that many suppliers grew from being reward suppliers to being general consultancies. Their heritage may therefore be important in their provision of certain types of reward. Most suppliers of reward and recognition have roots and expertise in one or more of the following sectors:

- merchandise;
- travel;
- gift cards;
- event management;
- training and skills development;
- consumer sales promotion.

If you know that the majority of your PIP requires the distribution of merchandise then it makes sense to choose a supplier with that specific type of background. If you are aware that your PIP will result in a series of overseas travel events as the main reward then it would be better to look at incentive travel suppliers to deliver the rewards element. It is unlikely that a supplier within the skills development sector will have the logistical skills to run a series of national events, for example. So some probing and research are necessary when purchasing reward and recognition suppliers to discover who might have the right mix of skills to deliver the best solution for your programme.

Budgeting strategy

Budgeting for a reward or recognition programme is unlike buying stock or property. In essence you are buying a series of connected services with a contingency for rewards that is only an estimate. If human behaviour were predictable we would not need to have programmes to encourage the right behaviours. Compliance would simply happen. For that reason some flexibility is always required when drafting and agreeing reward budgets. No sponsor would complain if the participants achieved over 90 per cent engagement as a result of the programme, as this level of performance would deliver many times the productivity that the rewards in such a programme would cost.

In Chapter 12 we examine briefly the implications of managing cross-border programmes and whether it is possible to have an effective recognition and reward scheme on a global basis. It is also worth looking at how easy or difficult it may be to manage reward events overseas, which often come out of reward programmes for the very highest achievers.

International aspects

12

It is tempting to believe that only your market runs reward and recognition schemes or, at the very most, just the English-speaking world. We have alluded to UK and US corporate programmes throughout this book. But performance improvement programmes (PIPs) are a global phenomenon in the same way that advertising or marketing is. Here are some examples.

SNCF, the French national railway system, needed to introduce more confident usage of its new customer ticketing system, SOCRATES, and at the same time train its 7,000 staff to sell up when being asked for tickets and make an effort to be more customer-friendly. A performance improvement programme was devised, which scored 30 per cent of performance on knowledge of the system and 70 per cent on ticket sales achievement. Nine key objectives were identified as part of a balanced scorecard approach, such as starting a conversation, offering alternatives and talking to customers while the tickets were being issued. Performance was monitored through the database and through mystery shoppers.

Rewards were offered at the time via a printed catalogue, and the 23 rail regions were leagued to ensure that teams were pitched like for like to qualify for the major rewards. Levels of upgraded ticket sales showed improvement in most regions, but more importantly there was an identifiable improvement in customer satisfaction with the way customer queries were handled and the level of technical fluency with the new system.

Carl Zeiss Italiana provides independent opticians in Italy with optical products and supports opticians with high-prestige and designer-branded wearables. To establish a channel of communication with its most valuable business partners Carl Zeiss created a recognition club with three levels of membership based on sales and the number of fully trained Carl Zeiss retail staff.

At the top level, VIP members receive a silver-plated membership card in a leather holder, which acts as a 'credit card' so they can purchase reward items through the online club secretariat. VIP members also qualify for an annual prestigious event overseas, such as Monte Carlo, Venice or Capri, along with their partners. The total hosted group is around 50 people, and partners are included. Membership of the Carl Zeiss Club is perceived as so desirable that some stockists display a certificate of their status in the public areas of their showroom, with photographs of them enjoying Carl Zeiss hospitality in exotic locations.

Germany first introduced incentive schemes into its statutory health system in 1989. Individuals were offered gift card payments for dental treatments if patients attended regularly for check-ups. Since then many other health services have been introduced to the principles of PIPs – research, skills, communication and incentive – to encourage relevant, preventative sessions, with the overall aim of reducing costs within the health service and promoting better well-being.

These examples show that the principles of well-run performance improvement programmes are managed not just by US and UK brands and their consultancies. Germany is particularly strong in programmes based on job competence. France tends to take the sales promotion route and emphasizes exotic overseas group events. Poland has a number of excellent team-building consultancies. Group events are the end reward for internal performance improvement. As overseas travel is relatively expensive per head, international travel is rare in Eastern Europe. The United States is probably the world leader in motivation programme concepts, having had some 70 years' experience of managing such schemes since the end of the Second World War in 1945.

PIPs are universal promotional tools to assist in the improvement of individuals' performance in the workplace. But what are the specific issues in attempting to run programmes that cross borders and often need to be run in different languages?

Multi-country programmes

Widely dispersed sales or operational teams can benefit from reward and recognition programmes, as they provide an unusual, international channel for communication between individuals, especially if people are being ranked in order and have to compete with each other.

Rolls-Royce Motor Cars Limited is a case in point. Compared with mainstream automotive manufacturers they sell relatively few units per year and have a global distribution that peaks in such places as London, Dubai and Los Angeles for reasons to do with the density of wealth in those conurbations. The expected reward mechanism for unit sales is gift vouchers. However, these rewards tend to be country- or retailer-specific. The question is what reward could be offered on a global basis but for local redemption.

Amazon gift cards or iTunes credits are one answer, as they can be redeemed online virtually anywhere in the world. But on closer inspection only certain types of product are available and, in particular, downloadable credits are the only ones that are offered globally. Another approach could be to examine hotel gift cards for a well-established international chain. Marriott for example has a product that can be redeemed in properties around the world for accommodation, spa and restaurant services, but you need to be careful that it has an outlet close to the domicile of all the winning participants. If a winner has to pay to travel 500 miles simply to redeem a voucher for 100 credits, it is probably not going to be perceived as an effective reward.

Some suppliers claim to offer a global reward mechanism for global campaigns, but as you might expect there are a number of restrictions on what can be offered:

- Electronic and electrical goods are barred from some countries owing to trade tariffs. The power system also needs to be compatible.

- Many countries do not allow alcohol to be imported without strict controls.

- Food items may be restricted for religious or health and safety reasons.

- Cash in the form of traveller's cheques or similar instruments will be subject to exchange controls.

- Some colours of items such as black, white or red may be deemed offensive to the local culture.

In the Rolls-Royce scenario it was clear that the rewards could not be tangibles that needed to be sent halfway around the world. The cost of sending specific items would be prohibitive, even if we could identify acceptable gifts that could be mailed to all the target countries. The solution was a series of events.

It was agreed that the very top achievers per league would be invited to London to stay at the Savoy and then on to Crewe, in the north of England, for a factory visit to the Rolls-Royce plant. The next level down qualified for a hosted overnight stay at a five-star hotel in their home country. At the lowest level, participants would receive items online that could be digitally downloaded up to a certain limit. In this way we managed to achieve a tiered reward system that not only suited the profile of the winners but was relatively easy to administer.

Language issues

The corporate language of Rolls-Royce Motor Cars Limited was English, as you might expect. This meant that all the communication could be in English on the basis that employees around the world would expect this from a British firm. Part of the employee contract was to have a good level of business English to be able to function effectively within the organization.

Another issue for international programme planners to deal with is therefore whether promotional material should be translated into local languages if it is being read and reviewed in local countries to have the best impact. As usual you should do your research and respond to the needs of the local market. Many years ago we were given the task of developing and rolling out a retail training course for Esso forecourt staff about maintaining tidy displays of product and merchandise around the area where customers came in to pay for their petrol. The original drafts were done in English as printed flipcharts with supporting cartoon characters to dramatize the main points. The parent company was Exxon

Mobil, with headquarters in Irving, Texas. We determined that most of the participants in the learning programme would be East European and of relatively low educational attainment. It would be unreasonable to expect them to absorb skills messages in English. The materials were therefore translated into several local languages and delivered locally in their own language by their local manager.

Concept transfer

A major US corporation ran a very successful peer-to-peer recognition programme in mainland United States, which offered gift cards at the basic level and an all-expenses trip to the factory at the main office. The very top qualifiers who had demonstrated the highest levels of achievement against corporate values were then taken off to Miami for a three-day cruise with their families. By all accounts it was a lavish programme and very well received both by the winning participants and by those who did not win, as it showed a very positive commitment to the idea of internal recognition.

It was agreed that the scheme should then be 'exported' around the world within the subsidiaries in the hope that the performance could be replicated. The same graphic designs were used, including the tell-tale US typeface, with all the text simply translated by an agency into 17 local languages. The English name of the programme was 'Theory into Practice', which had a particular relevance to the US advertising campaign at the time. When this was translated into Spanish the title of the programme became 'La teoria aplicada a la practica'. At first glance the translation was perfectly adequate, as it translated exactly what the English said. But in marketing terms it came across as a little awkward, and no one had any knowledge outside the United States of the relevant consumer advertising to which the theme referred. In addition there was a tinted photograph of the Miami cruise ship on the front cover. Unfortunately this particular top reward was not offered to the global participants owing to cost, and a more local reward was arranged.

When the scheme was cascaded down to the global subsidiaries they were somewhat perplexed by it. The gift cards being offered could be redeemed only in Sears outlets, and there was no mention of what the major rewards were. It later transpired that the senior local country manager was supposed to organize 'something similar' to the Miami cruise for the local market but had never got the briefing note or information about how much was supposed to be spent on it or, of great importance, who would be paying for it. This was truly a case of being global and acting global.

In addition many of the local employees in such places as Greece and Bulgaria carried out their daily tasks in offices of fewer than 20 people, rather than the hundreds and sometimes thousands of employees in each of the stateside offices. A peer-to-peer scheme needs a minimum level of employees, as otherwise the ideas dry up very quickly and the programme becomes a white elephant. It was clear that the programme was not fit for purpose.

In contrast Fiat Cars in Europe ran an accessories campaign to encourage dealership employees to promote winter accessories during the cold weather of the European winter. A planning meeting was held at their offices in Turin to which all the European marketing managers were invited. The Italian marketing team presented some visuals of promotional materials plus a suggested mechanism for calculating additional sales and some new shots of the branded accessories being sold. Local country marketing managers were then asked to reinvent the programme for their own country using bespoke artwork and campaign headlines. If they felt they did not need to have any printed material, it was not essential. It would be up to them to decide. In essence all the central marketing team wanted was compliance to run a programme featuring winter accessories during this particular period and to report back on the numbers. This is a good example of being global but acting local and letting the local market interpret how to go about it.

Destination choices for overseas travel events

In Chapter 8 we discussed the logic of choosing relevant destinations for outbound employee celebration events with the assumption that they were all travelling from the same country. But if there is a mixed-nationality audience of participant winners they will all be approaching your chosen destination from different parts of the globe. This provides a number of cultural and logistical challenges.

Culture

It is dangerous to assume that just because employees all work for the same organization they will be comfortable with the same treatment. For many employees in less developed countries overseas travel is an unheard-of luxury. Many employees do not have a passport, and there may be government restrictions on participants being able to fly anywhere overseas without significant bureaucracy and form filling. It may also be the case that they or members of their family will need to lodge sums of money with the authorities before they are even allowed to accept the travel tickets. It should be noted that even the cost of an economy flight to a nearby country could represent a year's remuneration for some employees, so such offers come with a halo effect of other feelings about the programme, especially if they feel they are not paid enough to do their day job.

Food and accommodation can cause specific issues when cultures clash. It is not unknown for subcontinent and Chinese winners of global campaigns to travel with a supply of local food, not realizing that at most border crossings they will be asked to complete a declaration stating that they are not importing foodstuffs of certain types.

In some cultures sleeping alone is a very rare occurrence, and often winning groups of participants from less developed countries will sleep together in the same room at the hotel, leaving their own luxury rooms untouched for the duration of their stay.

The provision of alcohol is common for Western groups and would be expected at all the evening meals. Other cultures do not have a history of alcohol consumption, either because of cost or because of religion. Some thought needs to be applied to offering alcohol at mixed-nationality or cross-cultural events. If in doubt it is advisable to avoid serving alcohol so as not to offend certain categories of participants.

Men and women are often separated socially in the Middle East and other parts of the world for cultural reasons. This needs to be considered when planning for briefing sessions, conferences, cocktail parties and mealtimes with a mixed-nationality group. Chaperoning still exists as a concept in many parts of the world, so you may need to be prepared to change the arrangements to suit the participants. It is not uncommon in some parts of the world for meals to be served sitting in groups on the floor rather than at table. We should not assume that everyone eats at a table.

There are a number of useful agencies and consultancies that offer courses and advice about dealing with cultural differences in businesses and organizations. If you find you are managing global participants on a regular basis and hosting them for events it is well worth seeking advice on a professional level.

Logistics

Most global organizations are based in the large conurbations of the United States and Europe. By default these are also the places that are best served by global airlines. In the developed West people become accustomed to having easy access to international flights, even if they have to connect through a hub, but for many global participants simply getting to the hub airport may take several days of logistical planning. You need to find out who the travelling participants are before making final decisions on central destinations, as difficulties in travel could result in many participants not being able to take part.

It is not unusual to invite the winning participants' partners to prestigious end-of-year celebration events. However, in many cultures it may not be the married partner who travels to the event. Often an invitee will travel with a same-sex relative. This has a number of logistical implications from invitations and joining instructions to accommodation, dining arrangements and paying for extras when they check out.

Leadership styles differ around the world, and this may affect the hosting of winners' groups with a global mix of participants. The UK tends to have a casual leadership model where leadership changes depending on the task being undertaken. In Germany there tends to be a strict hierarchy of leadership, with consensus being channelled through a clear leader. In Asia there are normally several people of high status who collectively make the main decisions for the group. This may sound abstract, but it can cause difficulties if the event organizers are asking for cooperation with timings and changes to the event schedule. There may not be one single leader, so asking for agreement to change things may require more time than you think.

Do global programmes work?

It is tempting to assume that, once devised, a local country reward or recognition programme can be rolled out to the rest of the world by simply undertaking translations and changing the reward mechanism. As we have seen there are a number of complexities that make this an unlikely option.

Even concepts of loyalty to an employer and engagement with fellow workers do not easily transfer across all cultures, even if human motivation is the same. Cultural differences with regard to social interaction and deference within a business context suggest that the best way forward is to brief local teams well on the purpose behind such programmes and allow them to work out how to implement them locally for themselves. There is no need to follow the theme or design of the central scheme, as the origination costs are minimal when compared with the costs of a global programme.

International schemes are not the only category of programme planning that requires some element of common sense and mid-campaign feedback when resolving difficult issues. In Chapter 13 we examine some of the likely scenarios where things go wrong and the programme needs to be remedied. No amount of planning can remove the possibility that messages will be misunderstood, rewards will not be delivered on time and some parts of the organization may simply not be supporting the programme for a variety of reasons.

Troubleshooting reward and recognition

13

It would be simplistic to think that, once launched, your reward or recognition scheme is going to work perfectly, that you will get 100 per cent engagement and that organizational performance will soar to heights never achieved before. All reward and recognition programmes rely on the active and positive contribution of the participants, who are all human and as such do not always behave in the way that you might expect. There are also a number of technical and logistic problems lying in wait for every programme planner. In this chapter we examine what could and does go wrong and how to fix things. All performance improvement programmes (PIPs) are dynamic projects that need to be monitored and adjusted while they are in use to get the most returns from them. If you think you can launch a programme and then leave it alone, it is unlikely to work well and deliver the returns you have promised.

Launching your programme

The most common fault when launching programmes is not to give them enough promotion. Internal or people initiatives tend to come well down the list of priorities when it comes to senior management support and endorsement. There is often a reluctance to spend budget on gaining acceptance for the new initiative, as budget-holders are focused on the possible reward pay-outs and the consequences of a potential overspend if performance is higher than anticipated. The mind tells you that higher performance than expected is a good thing, but the heart still feels that a large budget is being overspent on participants whose core task is to do things to the best of their abilities. A PIP with rewards can sometimes be viewed as an unnecessary expense.

Critics need to be reminded that publicly quoted organizations with a higher-than-average engagement score experienced a 28 per cent earnings per share (EPS) growth rate compared with firms with a low engagement score, which showed a decline in EPS of 11.2 per cent (Gebauer, 2008).

What would be the best way to launch a new scheme? To get extensive buy-in you will need to demonstrate the system in group briefings, face to face with the participants. This series of briefings will start with the senior team, who need to display total confidence in how it works and what participants have to do. Even if the senior team are not due to receive anything from the programme they need to be enthusiastic ambassadors for it from the very first day. Participants can be highly intuitive to any possible suggestion that the programme is not fully endorsed by the budget-holders. Their response is likely to be withdrawal, and so the possibility of full engagement ebbs away.

During the team supervisor or manager sessions there should be a section that deals with typical objections with model answers so that leaders are prepared for any negative feedback from their potential participants. In any organization there will always be naysayers who will undermine any new initiative to change the way things are. People are natural defenders of the status quo. Have your objections already worked out so that by the end of your sessions there are no reasons left why non-participation could be an option.

Ensure you have a feedback mechanism in place in the early days and weeks to respond to any misperceptions of how the scheme works and what its main features are. This could be an e-mail or voice call sample follow-up so that any unexpected amendments can be introduced quickly. With even the most careful planning there will always be errors and misunderstandings about how things work, so if it is an important glitch it needs to be addressed immediately rather than some months down the line when participants are not taking part because something is not quite right.

Most people need to be told things several times before they start to get involved or even take notice. You need to treat a new reward and recognition programme like a new product, discuss it fully beforehand, advertise it well, organize endorsements at every opportunity, and give early examples of who is using the scheme well and how it is being used. Most important of all, provide examples on internal media of early adopters and what they have earned in credits as a result of getting involved. It may be appropriate to offer 'double credits' (a fast-start technique) for the first month simply to draw attention to the benefits of participation at an early stage.

Using your back-end database, examine which groups or divisions are not as involved as others and step up your central communications to find out why. In most cases it is because the people work in off-site or remote parts of the organization or their manager has a particular issue with the style or administration of the system. It may be that the people were absent from the initial briefings and therefore do not feel confident enough with their team members to push the programme forward. Refresher launch sessions could easily be arranged to redress the balance and push up the levels of engagement. These sessions could be fronted by early adopters and business unit champions to emphasize the point that the programme is for the benefit of the participants as well as the organization so should not be viewed as yet another key task that people are required to carry out along with all their other daily tasks. Above all communication and collaboration should be fun rather than a chore.

If the scheme is professionally managed it is likely that there will be a blog element within the online website, which enables the sponsor to initiate discussions about some of the system features, with live feedback from around the organization as to how the scheme is being used. Such conversations need to be started and prompted by people within internal communications to ensure the conversations do not die down after a few days. Like a developing story from a popular journalist, the communication needs to be often, well informed and engaging so that participants feel this is something to do with them and not simply another organizational initiative.

Dealing with rewards

Once the scheme is under way and has gained some traction, by which we mean an engagement rate of 60 per cent or more, however you define engagement, the first sticking points are likely to be to do with the administration of the rewards. It is important that any rewards are distributed as soon as possible and to the right people. There will be a default option to send the rewards directly to individuals into their personalized reward accounts online, but in some cases managers may request the opportunity to be seen to be handing over the rewards at team briefings so that they can underline the purpose of the scheme and encourage others to do the same. Sending the rewards to individuals when the manager is expecting to use them in the next team briefing can be very damaging to the credibility of the programme with the manager and could result in the manager failing to support the scheme or similar schemes in future.

If rewards are being supplied automatically by a third party, check on how well the rewards are distributed. Most gift card and merchandise suppliers will have signed a service level agreement (SLA) that states they will deliver the rewards within a set number of days, or even hours if they are digitally based. Ask to see proof-of-delivery schedules statistics so that you can monitor delivery in the early days of the scheme so that you are sure that participants are receiving rewards as promised in a timely manner.

If the rewards are activity-based, such as leisure events or sporting event tickets, do your research to make sure that the redeemed tickets are actually for the events requested and that any bespoke events were delivered in a professional manner. As programme planners do not usually qualify for rewards they may never have the experience of receiving the rewards themselves, and so personal knowledge of the rewards administration may be low. It is one thing to brief a third party about what needs to be done but quite another to know that it is being done on a consistent and regular basis.

In the case of a group travel incentive it is best practice to undertake a site inspection at the destination before the group event is to take place to check that the proposed logistics work, that the restaurants to be used are appropriate and that the costs are still in line with the budget. A complete, hour-by-hour plan can then be drawn up to allocate tasks to the organizing team so that the group are treated like the top performers they are.

There are few people who can forget poor planning and ill-suited venues if the event is a reward. Forward planning is a key part of the reward delivery. Post-event, an online survey can be organized to find out what went right and more importantly what went wrong. Learning from mistakes, however small, will help your planning team to build up an expertise in running sought-after, celebratory events and something you can use in the next promotional message about the following year's programme.

If items are to be sent out to individuals' homes or workplaces it is false economy not to pay for some kind of recorded or special delivery, even if the item is not very valuable. Goods sent through the mail go astray in apartment blocks and office reception areas every day. Nothing is more frustrating for a winning participant than having to prove to the administration team that the much prized item of merchandise never arrived and therefore the programme should send out another one. If you have hundreds of winners in your scheme, not paying for proof of receipt could be an expensive mistake.

Hybrid reward and recognition systems

The administration and reward parts of almost all PIPs are very similar. There is a natural tendency to add more features to an existing programme rather than create a new one, but it is usually a false economy, as the result after a few years is often a programme that is trying to do too much and becomes confusing for the participants. The result will be falling engagement levels and eventually abandonment of the programme by the participants until a new one is invented that takes things back to basics again.

A peer-to-peer recognition scheme is an automated way to say thank-you to colleagues for doing a good job. If you add an ideas or suggestion scheme, using the same entry point for participants, it very soon becomes complex. Should the thank-yous be linked to saving money or generating revenue as in the ideas scheme? Should the ideas scheme have different rewards to the recognition programme? Should you have a performance report that provides both sets of activity, and how should those reports be passed on to the respective line managers? Anyone who has tried to make sense of a key performance indicator (KPI) report will understand the issue.

It is clear that, if separate programmes are run, participants can easily identify which is which and therefore how each scheme should be used. For example, 'Eureka' could be the brand name of the ideas scheme and 'Thanks' could be the brand name of the recognition programme. If the schemes are separated in this way, participants are fully aware that they are strategically different and their purpose is clear.

Abuse of corporate programmes and errors

For the vast majority of participants, taking part in a motivation programme is something that is both challenging and rewarding for all the right reasons of alignment and having exceptional effort rewarded, but from time to time there may be participants who exploit the system for unfair gain. Within employee programmes it tends to be collusion, either between peers or between peers and supervising managers, to defraud the organization of rewards. In sales schemes it tends to be individuals claiming for sales that do not exist or falsifying quality reports in order to validate a certain level of sales.

Occasionally there will be a mistake in the drafting of the rules that allows participants to claim rewards to which they are not strictly entitled. This can occur in the instance of participants changing their role or leaving the organization completely and then perhaps returning at a later date with a different job role. In large organizations, such things happen. To avoid such instances undermining the programme in the eyes of the other participants it is important to examine the rules carefully and discuss with line managers beforehand whether specific rules could be written in to avoid exploitation of this kind.

One of the most common mistakes in rules writing is to omit reference to the tax treatment of the rewards. In most Western jurisdictions rewards are taxable when received by the individual. Unless the sponsor is prepared to cover the grossed-up cost of the rewards (contribute the tax levied on the reward and the tax on the tax!) the individual must pay this tax at the end of the financial year and include it in any tax declarations. This can be particularly onerous if partners are included in events, as tax becomes liable on the cost of both parties, not just the employee. It is not unknown for some organizations to have to pay out fines in the millions to settle a claim by the tax authorities for old schemes for which tax was never accrued.

Another frequent error is to forget to mention that no cash substitutes will be offered. The issue here is that many sponsors pay a reduced amount for rewards on the understanding that they will buy in bulk or in advance to secure the promoted rewards. The rewards cost less than face value, and so claimants would get less reward than they felt they were entitled to. Events in particular need to be paid for in advance in many cases, and so if participants choose not to join the event group their reward money is lost in attrition fees and any bulk purchasing arrangements. The cash is simply no longer available to pay out.

It needs to be accepted that gift cards may be purchased at say 90 per cent of their retail value, so if participants wanted the money instead they would receive their reward less the bulk discount.

Scheme transfer to a new supplier

Reward and recognition programmes are significant items of expenditure if undertaken in a professional manner. Owing to their cost most formal programmes are put up for tender on a regular basis just like any other important purchase. Negotiations are organized by the buying or procurement team, and suppliers are compared with each other to quantify which provider has the best-quality product. Most buying teams put such tenders out for pitch every three years, and some may have a policy of checking the market offering more frequently than that. Leaving aside for now the question of price, there are some issues with supplier offerings that need to be kept in mind.

At the heart of all effective programmes is the software code that administers the scheme. It is normally a bespoke platform, which is then further customized to suit the needs of the sponsor. It can take several months to enable the system to be compatible with the sponsor's internal reporting routines, not to mention the front-end visual design, which needs to fit in with the sponsor's brand and the theme of the programme. Changing suppliers can be an expensive undertaking, as the bespoke code will have already been paid for. If a new supplier is chosen the code will have to be rewritten. Such costs are not insignificant, depending on the complexity of what you want the code to do. There has to be a compelling reason to change your supplier and, if so, you need to be prepared for a hiatus in the scheme while the switch-over can happen and the new support team is fully briefed on all the oddities of the current system.

The participants themselves will have to be accommodating, as the transfer of individual files is not straightforward, especially if the new supplier is using a different code language or support system. The turnround of rewards is likely to be disrupted as files are exchanged and software routines are checked. The new supplier may not use the same gift card system as the former supplier for reasons of habit, cost or reliability, so there will inevitably be some disruption in the service levels of reward delivery. Clearly, changing suppliers is a common occurrence for organizations and cannot be ruled out for ever.

My cautionary note is that it is not as easy as it would appear to brief a new supplier, and perhaps only one in five pitches results in suppliers of recognition and reward programmes being changed. If your buyers have discovered an exciting new supplier in the field, they should be applauded, but be prepared for considerable disruption to engagement levels while the new supplier beds in. Check carefully that the switch-over is not solely based on costs, as it could prove to be an expensive mistake in the long run.

The participant is always right

When you examine your strategy for reward and recognition, one element should be uppermost in your mind. What are the expectations of the participants, and how can the programme planner best deliver what they want?

A PIP is only as good as the improved performance it can generate from the participant database. There are many technical issues, from listening to the research, to the development of the software code, to the effective promotion of the messages and the delivery of the rewards. You will be trying to do something that is difficult and often frustrating, but the main criterion for success is how the participants feel in terms of their attitude to the organization and by how much their performance has improved as a result.

You need to build in mechanisms to pulse-check how the participants feel about the programme and what they suggest in terms of improvement, and be prepared on a regular basis to have your assumptions challenged and change the system if you need to. No workforce stays the same, year after year. As the economy waxes and wanes so does the profile of the people who work for the organization. Their age range will change and if you acquire new organizations so will their tastes and expectations. You need to be prepared to modify your programme to suit the new market of participants.

An effective reward and recognition programme run professionally and on budget can make a significant contribution to job satisfaction and a feeling of well-being for most employees. In turn it provides the working environment for good team management to flourish and for organizations to make progress and get things done because everyone is aligned to the three or four core values that make the entire team successful.

Higher performance and better engagement are the ultimate goals of a well-run reward and recognition programme. Without such schemes many workplaces are much the poorer, both in the quality of what they produce and in the experiences of those who work there.

The future of reward and recognition

14

Important people have said many memorable things about the future. What they said is remembered mostly because they were wrong. In 1943 an IBM executive suggested that there would be no demand for more than five computers, globally, in the years to come. The one I like best is often attributed to Ken Olsen, former president and chairman of Digital Equipment Corporation (DEC), from 1977: 'There is no reason anyone would want a computer in their home.' Hindsight is a wonderful thing. It is easy to look back years later and enjoy identifying all those leading businesspeople who got things wrong.

However, predicting the future is easy if you know you will not have to defend what you said. For that reason, when I think about the future of employee reward and recognition, I feel secure in the knowledge that whether I am right or wrong there will be no consequences for me.

My review of the future starts with the internet. The internet and the World Wide Web have changed the way employees, distributors and customers engage with each other in a significant way. It was not until the mid-1990s that large organizations were even able to send messages and large documents on a global basis in the space of a few seconds to their colleagues and business partners around the world. Now, the facility to be in contact, constantly and instantly, for an organization is a given and has changed the way employees interact with their line managers and the organization as a whole. The speed and complexity of this interchange have rewritten the rules about how to behave in organizations of all sizes and especially about how to run effective employee reward and recognition programmes.

Schemes can be proposed, discussed, developed and launched online without the need for long internal meetings and political posturing. The incoming working generation seems to prefer it this way and see the world of work as somewhere to learn in and communicate rather than somewhere to comply with, so in future that is the way it will be.

Peer-to-peer, not top-down

The most striking change in organizational life since the 1990s, following the introduction of intranets and the internet, has been the shift from 'command-and-control' structures, or top-down as they are sometimes known, to peer-to-peer systems. Within recognition programmes, for example, we have already seen the revival of suggestion schemes as a direct result of the new ease of administration in collecting and assessing ideas online, recognizing individuals on an automatic basis and then rewarding them with credits in a personal account that they can save or redeem at will. Little intervention from mid-level managers is required, apart from consultation on making any process changes or the analysis of participant feedback. There should be no reason any more why ideas programmes should be cumbersome or time-consuming or await decisions from on high now that intranets are used by virtually everyone who is employed.

Acceptance of peer-to-peer decision-making systems is as much about the rise of the Millennials and technology as it is about attitudes to open communication. Although we still live in a world run by pre-internet executives who distrust IT and online communication in general and still resist many efforts to make communication easier, things are changing. We are seeing new paradigms in the use of communications technology within organizations as the Millennials and their successors, with their three or four communication devices, take up positions of executive power, even in middle management.

Stories about CEOs who cannot use a computer for e-mail or who are unable to complete a spreadsheet will be a thing of the past. They will no longer be viewed as charming networkers or buccaneering mavericks, but simply out of touch. In future all senior people will be expected to know how their devices work, what the organization's IT system can deliver and how best to get in touch with people and gather data in the most efficient way possible, as and when organizational problems arise.

Let's examine the four stages of performance improvement programmes (PIPs) again, but this time from the viewpoint of what the future may hold and how things may change in the years to come when it comes to reward and recognition.

Participant research

In future, rather than have a six-week or more run-up to a research project to consider changing the recognition programme, proposals and discussions could be held online, across the various categories of employee or distributor. The most favourable amendments could then be tested online with a sample group of participant types and then analysed online in order to come up with the optimum package of changes. A concept can be tested online before rolling it out to the entire organization. The executive will be required only to sign off on the budget, as the research will largely write the structure of the new programme to be implemented and the pilot group will already love the scheme. So what is there to discuss?

Algorithms could be used to check that participant suggestions comply with the organization's values using text recognition and therefore be rejected if the pattern of text in the proposal does not match the values the organization is seeking to exploit. There would be no need for line manager intervention or lengthy policy meetings. In the same way, collecting preferences about individuals' reward choices will reveal a pattern whereby participants can be offered rewards in future for which they have shown a preference in earlier schemes or from their profile. It could work in a similar way to Amazon, where you build up a personal history of book or music purchases.

Skype or YouTube could be used more widely as a means to get research feedback from younger participants, who might feel less comfortable about filling in forms, talking directly to researchers and having things written down but would be happy to answer questions in a video context, perhaps with a few colleagues in view at the same time, so that some discussion and debate could be created. The rise of instant social media apps such as Snapchat and WhatsApp suggests that the Millennials are very comfortable with using visuals and editing apps to make their point in an engaging manner.

Research reports use a variety of graphic devices to communicate data to the sponsor. It is possible to have the same data presented in various formats depending on the participant categories. Rather than a single written report for senior executives, the research findings could be posted online in several suitable formats, determined automatically by who is looking at them, so as to communicate what is key to the participant category rather than needing to be dissected and interpreted by the programme planner and then distributed. A short video of someone talking about the programme is often more valuable than a bar chart or a diagram in getting the main point across.

Skills development

We have already seen skills training moving online rather than mostly being delivered live in classroom situations. It is likely that most process and technical training in the future will be delivered online by default, unless some policy or cost discussion is required. But this can also be online in the form of video-conferencing and texting under certain circumstances.

The developments in smartphone technology suggest that many types of participant will be able to take a short 'skills course' while commuting or at home in order to build up their knowledge in their downtime. Even within the office it is possible to broadcast skills information via the intranet and track those who engaged with the information. In this way managers can track the levels of skills development taken up by their teams and the consequent improvement in efficiency. Rather than an assessment of skills needs face to face every year in the appraisal or similar internal meetings, skills development can be triggered by the database telling the individual and the manager who needs to be briefed on what, so that the team becomes more efficient as a whole.

In the future the role of the trainer will become more about online video presentations, packaging up short tactical pieces and trainee analysis than addressing groups of people face to face in offices with visual aids. Trainers who can interpret data, borrow key visuals from the internet and mix and match multimedia will become more useful than those who can stand up on their feet and deliver technical stories for a couple of hours.

Communication

As organizations begin to understand the positive impact of social media and how to protect themselves from malicious use, it is clear that organizational social media will develop to provide a reliable and secure communication hub for employees and their business partners. The organization's social medium will therefore become the main way individuals communicate with each other in the future, with e-mail reserved for formal proposals and documents.

The explosive growth in applications means that most organizations will be producing and issuing closed organizational apps for use by their employees and distributors rather than referring participants to websites, as most corporate websites are far too clunky and cumbersome to be able to deal with the mechanics of what employees most need to know.

Developments in low-cost animation will mean that expensive 'talking heads' on video could be replaced with avatars that reflect better the organization's values and can become apolitical presenters of programmes and initiatives. Currently being used in conferences as synthetic presenters, they could provide a trusted conduit for getting new messages across to an audience within closed intranets who perhaps are less interested in hearing what executives have to say than you might think.

The printed brochure as the main means to promote a new programme will disappear, owing to its expense and its anti-ecological implications. As there will be a number of variants of the programme details, depending on the category of participant, it no longer makes sense to print physical brochures that may well get recycled as soon as they are distributed and read.

Regular updates on progress, for both reward and recognition, will be delivered digitally by text or its equivalent. If the wearables market continues to grow it may be that handsets become wristwatches or glasses, so promotional messages will always be available, even if the mobile or cellphone becomes obsolete in time. Although talk of microchips embedded in humans at birth sounds fanciful, most pet owners already accept this as a means of keeping their animals safe and in touch, so why not humans?

Rewards

Physical items of merchandise in most developed markets have already become digital credits within the space of just 20 years. What the future holds is not clear when it comes to incentivizing participants with rewards whenever they comply with the recognition or incentive programme.

There has been some movement towards activity and unique social events rather than specific items within groups of employees who do not need the rewards to make ends meet at the end of the month. It may be that in the future when money becomes simply an electric pulse in a server rewards will be a credit that can be applied in a variety of ways. Inspiring participants with the choice of reward has always been the brief of most programme planners. In the early days it was a printed catalogue, but today the value can be applied to almost any goods or service. If everyone is online, even rewards retailers, then we have to find other ways to be aspirational and unique.

One way forward could be to 'crowdsource' a unique event for a group of people who have expressed an interest in such an event. For example, a group of music fans may want to meet their teenage music hero, now in his 40s, who happens to be in New York in March. Participants who live locally and have expressed an interest in this now mature celebrity could be asked if they want to redeem their rewards for such an event. The same reward supplier then contacts the celebrity and asks for his best price to make himself available. If it all works out, everyone is happy.

The rise in gifting any rewards from programmes to worthy causes is modest but clear. In mature schemes many participants feel that receiving discretionary rewards for doing something they feel they should be doing anyway sits uncomfortably with them. By opting to donate their rewards to charity they feel they are giving back and helping those less fortunate than themselves. It would not be fanciful for a major organization to present its entire recognition programme with charitable rather than personal rewards as part of its corporate social responsibility (CSR) commitment to deserving causes.

If we are to believe the statistics about employees changing jobs every four years and more people having several jobs in the form of portfolio careers, there is an argument for rewards to be completely portable as well. It would make sense for reward suppliers to aggregate each individual's rewards under one personal account so that wherever individuals worked all their rewards could be stored in one account. This is not dissimilar to retirement planning, where all credits from past employment are stored in the individual's account rather than in the account of one employer. This could easily be done with such universal reward systems as Amazon credits, although as yet such credits are not global.

Time for rewards to go?

Promotional ideas all suit their time and environment. The rationale for having ideas and thank-you systems is based on the premise that participants will not do their best without some coaxing and promotion. These are discretionary activities that employees or distributors are not obliged to do. Arguably, even if they were contractual, it would be very hard to enforce this as a term of employment or as part of a business partner deal. The rewards are supplied in most cases to encourage compliance with a task that most people do not naturally carry out unless they are reminded of it.

It is quite reasonable to imagine that in the future the business case for higher engagement through recognition will be so compelling at the strategic level that it will become a core part of every manager's competence. One of every professional manager's KPIs would be to monitor the recognition system and ensure team members are aware of what is available and how it works and that all employees are expected to be involved with it. If this were to happen then the rewards element would disappear. Recognizing others and being recognized yourself for values-aligned behaviour should be a standard part of organizational life, as it brings so many benefits to the individuals' self-esteem and to the bottom line of the organization. It just makes good sense.

For the moment, though, while the organizational world adjusts itself to the internet, algorithms in consumer behaviour, smartphones, social media, wearables and avatars, one question to put would be whether we still need recognition and reward schemes to remind us to thank people for doing a good job, to provide ideas for improvement or to encourage higher sales.

I leave the last word to William James, the 19th-century US philosopher, writer and commentator: 'The deepest cravings in human nature is the craving to be appreciated.' How we meet this need with recognition programmes, with or without rewards, is still up for debate, whatever advances there may be in technology.

REFERENCES

Armstrong, Michael (2012) *Armstrong's Handbook of Human Resource Management Practice*, 12th edn, Kogan Page, London

Berlet, K Richard and Cravens, Douglas M (1991) *Performance Pay as a Competitive Weapon: A compensation policy model for the 1990s*, Wiley, New York

Bloom, BS *et al* (1956) *Taxonomy of Educational Objectives: The classification of educational goals*, Handbook I: *Cognitive Domain*, David McKay Company, New York

Csikszentmihalyi, Mihaly (2002) *Flow: The psychology of happiness: The classic work on how to achieve happiness*, Rider/Random House, London

Fisher, John G (2014) *Strategic Brand Engagement*, Kogan Page, London

Ford, Martin E (1992) *Motivating Humans*, Sage, Newbury Park, CA

Gebauer, Julie (2008) *Closing the Engagement Gap*, Penguin, New York

Guerin, Bernard (2009) *Social Facilitation*, Cambridge University Press, Cambridge

Herzberg, Frederick (1959) *The Motivation to Work*, Wiley, New York

Hull, Clark Leonard (1943) *Principles of Behavior: An introduction to behavior theory*, Appleton-Century-Crofts, New York

Human Capital Institute (2009) The value and ROI in employee recognition, briefing paper, http://www.hci.org

James, William ([1890] 1950) *Principles of Psychology*, vol 1, Dover, New York

Jeffrey, Scott (2004) The benefits of tangible non-monetary incentives, paper, University of Chicago Graduate Business School

Jensen, Michael C and Murphy, Kevin J (1990) It's not how much you pay, but how, *Harvard Business Review*, 68 (3) (May–June), 138–53

Kirkpatrick, Donald L and Kirkpatrick, James D (2009) *Evaluating Training Programs*, Berrett-Koehler, San Francisco, CA

Kohler, Heinz (1997) *Economic Systems and Human Welfare: A global survey*, South-Western, Cincinnati, OH

Kolb, Alice Y and Kolb, David A (2005) Learning styles and learning spaces: enhancing experiential learning in higher education, *Academy of Management Learning and Education*, 4 (2), pp 193–212

Latham, Gary P (2012) *Work Motivation: History, theory, research and practice*, Sage, Los Angeles, CA

Maslow, AH (1943) A theory of human motivation, *Psychological Review*, 50 (4), pp 370–96

Murray, Henry A ([1938] 2008) *Explorations in Personality*, Oxford University Press, Oxford

Phillips, Jack J (2011) *Return on Investment in Training and Performance Improvement Programs*, Routledge, London

Pink, Daniel H (2009) *Drive: The surprising truth about what motivates us*, Riverhead Books, New York

Rogers, Carl and Freiberg, H Jerome (1994) *Freedom to Learn*, Merrill, Columbus, OH

Schweyer, Allan (2010) The economics of engagement, available online from Incentive Research Foundation Resource Center, http://theirf.org/research/content/6000044/the-economics-of-engagement/

Smythe, John (2007) *The CEO: Chief engagement officer*, Gower Publishing, Burlington, VT

Towers Watson (2009) *Turbocharging Employee Engagement: The power of recognition from managers*, part 1: *The Engagement Engine*, April, Towers Watson, New York

Toynbee, Polly and Walker, David (2009) *Unjust Rewards*, Granta Publications, London

Vroom, Victor H ([1964] 1994) *Work and Motivation*, Jossey-Bass, San Francisco, CA

WorldatWork (2008) *Trends in Employee Recognition, 2008*, WorldatWork, Washington, DC

FURTHER READING

Ayres, I (2010) *Carrots and Sticks*, Bantam Books, New York

Dixon, Patrick (2007) *Futurewise*, Profile Books, London

Drucker, Peter (2011) *Managing for Results*, Routledge, London

Fargus, Peter (2000) *Measuring and Improving Employee Motivation*, Pearson, London

Fisher, John G (2008) *How to Run Successful Employee Incentive Schemes*, Kogan Page, London

Fisher, John G (2014) *Strategic Brand Engagement*, Kogan Page, London

Ford, Martin E (1992) *Motivating Humans*, Sage, Newbury Park, CA

Furnham, A (2014) *The New Psychology of Money*, Routledge, London

Kaplan, Ann R (1998) *Maslow on Management*, John Wiley & Sons, New York

Kohn, A (1999) *Punished by Rewards*, Houghton Mifflin, New York

Laffont, J-J and Martimort, D (2002) *The Theory of Incentives*, Princeton University Press, Princeton, NJ

Lewis, Richard D (1996) *When Cultures Collide*, Nicholas Brealey, London

Lidstone, John (1995) *Motivating Your Sales Force*, Gower, Aldershot

Maslow, Abraham H (1987) *Motivation and Personality*, 3rd edn, Harper & Row, New York

Nelson, Bob (2012) *1501 Ways to Reward Employees*, Workman, New York

Stewart, Thomas A (1998) *Intellectual Capital*, Nicholas Brealey, London

Thomson, K (1990) *The Employee Revolution*, Pitman Publishing, London

Vroom, Victor H (1995) *Work and Motivation*, Jossey-Bass, San Francisco

INDEX

Entries in *italics* denote information within a table.